AF531634

ADVERTISEMENT AND CONSUMER

ADVERTISEMENT AND CONSUMER

By

Prof. Basant Mehta

&

Anurag Mehta

DISCOVERY PUBLISHING HOUSE PVT. LTD.

NEW DELHI-110 002

First Published-2010

ISBN 978-81-8356-623-0

Published by:
DISCOVERY PUBLISHING HOUSE PVT. LTD.
4831/24, Ansari Road, Prahlad Street
Darya Ganj, New Delhi-110002 (India)
Phone: 23279245, 43764432 • Fax: 91-11-23253475
E-mail: parul.wasan@gmail.com
info@discoverypublishinggroup.com
Website: www.discoverypublishinggroup.com

Printed at:

Sachin Printers
Delhi

Preface

Advertising is an important marketing activity. Lot of time, money and energy is spent on development and publishing/broadcasting of advertisements (ads). Amid intensified competition it is a very challenging task to develop and communicate the whole advertising message in a convincing manner to achieve the desired advertising goals. For that purpose best and most effective ad copy should be used. In this book an effort has been made to find the most effective ad copy for different consumer products in three media channels namely newspaper, magazine and television. Besides that growth of ads and their contribution into sale has been studied in detail so the real assessment of advertising effectiveness has been made.

The book has been divided into six chapters. First chapter gives introduction of the study and explains the research methodology. The second chapter describes ad copy and explains the components and kinds of ad copy with examples in details. The third chapter deals with different ad copies relating to consumer durables and non-durables published in newspapers and their effect. The fourth chapter deals with different ad copies relating to consumer durables and non-durables published in magazines and their effect. While fifth chapter deals with different ad copies relating to consumer durables and non-durables broadcasted on television and their effect. The last sixth chapter expresses the findings of whole research study and draw conclusions from them. Suggestions for making effective ad copies have been given and for every product category appropriate and most effective ad copy has been recommended.

Prof. BASANT MEHTA
Dr. ANURAG MEHTA

Contents

1 Research Methodology

INTRODUCTION

Business organisations either produce a product or render any service. These products and services are meant for customers. So the management has to make their products or services, its features, qualities, benefits and availability known to the prospects. This task is done by advertising the product or service through different media.

Advertising can be better understood in two ways first from Marketing point of view and second from Communication point of view.

"Advertisement is Salesmanship in print."

—Laskar

> "Advertising is any paid form of non-personal presentation and promotion of ideas, goods or services by an identified sponsor."
>
> *—American Marketing Association*

> "Advertising is any form of paid non-personal presentation of ideas or services for the purpose of inducing people to buy."
>
> *—Wheeler*

These definitions clearly suggest that advertising is an important marketing activity that stimulates demand and contribute in sale. From the communication point of view it is said:

> "Advertising is controlled identifiable information and persuasion by means of mass communication media."

> "Advertising tells the consumers what's available, offers a parade of suggestions on how they may spend their money; and gives the freedom to accept or reject these options as they wishes."[1]

Advertising provides the communication link between someone with something to sell and someone who needs something. Advertisement (Ad) provides information to the persons who are seeking it. Advertising helps the consumers to make an intelligent choice. Through it, consumers are able to anticipate satisfaction, compare values, and do the shopping even before they go out of their homes. Advertising in general creates awareness and builds confidence, consumers tend to choose the product they know and trust.

> "Advertising is mass, paid communication, the ultimate purpose of which is to impart information, develop attitude and induce action beneficial to the advertiser—generally the sale of a product or service".
>
> —*Russel H. Colley*

The competition is very intensified in the field of consumer goods. Everyone is trying hard leaving no stone unturned to enhance the sale of his product. Whether it is big corporate houses like Parle and Raymond or the roadside bakeryman and tailor everyone in on move, they are all using ads for the benefit of their business.

Advertisement is not just an occasional activity that is used when the firm or the product is new or the sale shows declining trend. Ads are made frequently/ repeatedly as a routine business activity. Whether to advertise or not is not a question at all. The question that arise today is how to advertise more and more effectively to increase sales, to create new customers and to develop new markets.

Lot of time is devoted by the business officials planning, preparing and broadcasting the ads. If it succeeds company flourish but if it fails company dooms. So it is imperative to take full care and caution in advertising, conduct due research and investigation before making an ad copy. A very common fault resulting in failure of the ad is weakness in the copy. Weakness of copy means that the copy is not well planned and prepared according to the needs, desires, likings, taste and attitude of the consumers. Consumers react negatively to such weak copy. If the ad copy appeals weakly, the consumer will not be stimulated. Consequently, they will not patronize the product and the very purpose of advertising will go in vain. The ad copy should be such that it not only grab the attention of the readers or viewers but also encourage them to such an extent that they could not resist their temptation to purchase the product. Really ad copy is very significant and we have to study it in detail. It is important for the advertiser to know what are the traits the consumers are seeking in their product, what are the main features that really convince the potentials.

In this work the reactions of consumers about the various kinds of ad copy published in newspapers, magazines and broadcasted on television were studied in detail. Thereby, we comprehend which type of ad copies are more effective and really grab the attention of prospects and pushes them to buy the advertised products. Thereby, we will be in a better position to make ad more effective and fruitful to promote the sales.

REVIEW OF LITERATURE

It is said 'knowledge is key to success'. If one has sound knowledge of past he can take lessons from it and perform infallibly in present making his future rich. Similarly, in research the past studies and investigations can contribute to show the path where the work has been done, how much that work has contributed, what are the limitations. To develop and prosper the knowledge base perusal of literature directly or indirectly related to the proposed study has been made.

"I don't know what you are, I don't know your company, I don't know your Co.'s product, I don't know what your Co. stands for, I don't know your Co.'s customers, I don't know your Co.'s record, I don't know your Co.'s reputation. Now - what was it you wanted to sell me?"[2] Such typical questions are raised by the prospects whenever a salesman tries to sell a non-advertised packaged consumer product so it has become essential for the marketing-man to advertise his product. Today the market is quite well informed where one cann't carve a niche for oneself without advertising. The object of advertising is to make known and build confidence in the goods or commodities sold by salesman. The salesman thus approaches a prospect, who is already aware of goods through advertising and has the basic information about it. The salesman's job thus become easier.[3]

Advertising does any more things than just assisting the salesmen. "Advertising is intended to achieve predetermined objectives such as improved memorability, reinforcement of other promotion, change of attitudes or product sampling" (Burnett, 1997).[4] In other words the actual aim of advertising is not to sell but to induce people to try the product or service offered.[5] Walter made it clear that ads do not create demand but they stimulate demand for the advertised product. The latent desires are evoked through advertising messages.

R.C. Bhatia in his eminent work *Business Organisation and Management* mentioned that business firms advertise with one or more of the following objectives:

(1) Introduction of new products,

(2) Inducing potential customers to buy,

(3) Reminding users,

(4) Create brand image,

(5) Intimate customer about new uses of product,

(6) Highlight brand character,

(7) Dealer support and

(8) Trafficking retail trade.

A broader framework for understanding what advertising can do is provided by Sheth (1974). He describes four basic sequential functions of advertising:

(1) Precipitation i.e. to stimulate needs and wants and create general awareness,

(2) Persuasion through reasoning, convincing or argumentation,

(3) Reinforcement by making people feel good about their previous decisions to buy product, and

(4) Reminder by repetition of advertising message using minimal text.[7]

Up to now it is clear that what is advertising and what it is intended to do but how it works is explained

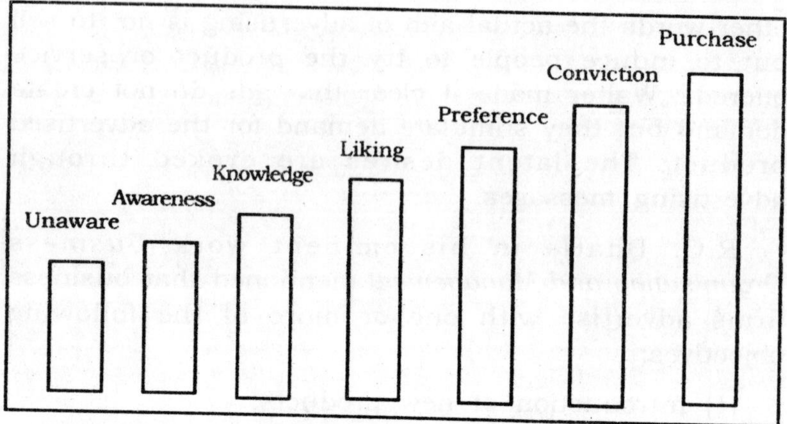

A Model for Predictive Measurements of Advertising Effectiveness

by *hierarchy of effects* model proposed by various researchers. One model that stood the test of time well was developed by Lavidge and Steiner (1961). Ads move consumers closer to buying a product step by step-from being unaware of a product to buying it.

At starting prospects are unaware of product's existence. The first two steps in the chain awareness and knowledge relate to information or ideas. The next two steps liking and preference develop favourable attitudes or feelings towards the product and the Final two steps conviction and purchase produce action i.e. the acquisition of the product.[8]

These three advertising functions can be compared with the classic psychological model which divides behaviour into three dimensions as:

(a) cognitive-intellectual, mental or rationed component,

(b) affective-emotional or feeling component,

(c) conative-motivational, striving component, treating objects as positive or negative goals.

This view is confirmed by Czinkota and Kotabe (2000) in their work on Marketing Management where they stated three main advertising aspects building awareness, creating favourable attitudes and maintaining customer loyalty.[9]

Consumer research, product research, market research, advertising research, sales research, distribution research, motivational research, industrial marketing research, international marketing research and market testing are the major types of marketing research. They benefits a lot in understanding consumer needs, buying motives and bases, improving product, increasing sales, discovering new markets, estimating demand, evaluating policies etc.[10]

Lucks *et al.* (1970) emphasized that research helps in making sales promotion efforts more effective. It helps in determining the best sales appeals of the products, the best ways of reaching the potential buyers and the most fruitful timing of promotion.[11]

Research provides the solid base for decision-making and planning. It broaden the understanding of marketing-man by providing factual informations. Research oriented approach is far better and objective than the intuitive approach in decision making relating to advertising (message content, media and budget).[12]

In an area of advertising the research is even more important as the ads are directed towards the consumers who's behaviour, attitude, likes, dislikes, preferences, habits, earnings are dynamic so the facts about prospects should be constantly updated (as often as information is available), and at least annually. Look for changes in age groups, for changes in income, spending pattern and particularly for changes in characteristics of users and owners, Durkee (1967) said this will make advertising effective and workable.[13]

Advertising research is very fruitful but it has its own limitations. Research can at the most provide a base for predicting future events. It may help in reducing the size of area of uncertainty. Research is passive and therefore, its use and effectiveness depend on the ability and judgement of the exclusive who use it. Many executives are not able to make use of and get the maximum value out of marketing research.[14] The executives have to develop a dynamic approach and incorporate changes in their advertising campaigns as per the findings and suggestions of the advertising research.

Sudha (2000) very clearly stated the scope of advertising research. Advertising Research is an area of marketing research, it undertakes a study relating to the preparation of ad copy (copy research), the media to be used (media research) and measurement of advertising effectiveness.[15]

Advertising being a communication activity must follow the principles of good communication. "The objective of communication may be defined as the passing of ideas and understanding from the sender to the target with the view to get the desired behavioural response from the later. . . . Effective communication, as such, might be accurate transmission and receipt thereof and its correct understanding. There are several elements in communication which can be evaluated to assess directly the effectiveness of communication. These elements are: clarity, adequacy, integrity and timing of communication."[16]

The ad copy should clearly convey the required advertising message to the target viewers or audience at the right time. "The aim of advertising is that it should be seen, read and acted upon. People must be able to look, like, learn and buy from a good copy of an ad for some product."[17]

Advertising agencies must develop an ad copy according to the objective of advertiser which can be:

(1) Closing an immediate sale (buy now because of price),

(2) Creating near-term sales by moving the prospect closer to a purchase (combating competitive claims),

(3) Building a long-range consumer franchise (establish brand recognition and acceptance),

(4) Contribute towards increased sales (convert non-users of the product type),

(5) Emphasizing a specific step which leads to a sale (induce prospects to sample the product),

(6) Imparting informations needed to close a sale (where to buy it),

(7) Building confidence in the company (past and present profit ability) and

(8) Building images (Product quality and corporate citizenship).[18]

Because of the great and growing similarity of products and multiplicity of strong brands, it is vital to build a *distinct brand personality* and engrave a sharply defined brand image on the consumer's consciousness.[19] By making such product differentiation the copywriter reduces the chance of substituting the product with other competitive products. The text of the copy must include a statement of exact product value that the ad will communicate to potential consumers. The heart of the creative message should be presented as a clearly defined brand advantage and benefit, one that is important enough to the target audience to serve as the power base around which the entire ad will develop.[20] The image we are creating should not be such that can be considered fake or sheer puffery.

David Foster (1975) of Colgate-Palmolive very rightly said:

> "I want ad be in good taste and *believable.* I am a strong believer in having products live upto their advertising. You must let the consumer know that you really care about the choice that he or she makes."[21]

The advertisement message and its presentation should be believable and trustworthy so that the prospects can be stimulated to try the product and get the claimed satisfaction. This will also develop the repeated buying in future.

Denis Higgins (19650 in *The Art of Writing Advertising* explained the importance of brevity and *conciseness.* He stated "Eyerything you write, everything on a page, every word, every graphic symbol, every shadow should further the message you are trying to convey".[22]

Copy should be only as long as necessary to complete the sales job. This means long copy is often appropriate only for the highly interested reader (such as people contemplating car purchase).[23] Unnecessary explanation and details should be avoided as most of the people do not have much time to go through the lengthy ad.

Commercials (TV ads) are so loaded with frills that the *message* becomes *buried under the giltter and glamour* of a tiny motion picture epic. A true selling commercial requires the writer to have a logical, disciplined, orderly mind. He must think first of the problem and eventually determine the solution.[24]

David Ogilvy, 'In Confession of Advertising Man' said:

> "I belong to the school which holds that a good ad is one which sells the product without drawing attention to itself. It should rivet the readers *attention to the product.* Instead of saying 'what a clever ad' the reader says 'I never knew that before. I must try this product'."[25]

Ancastasi (1964) and Starch (1954, 1961) in research studies showed that irrelevant, bizzare or arty illustrations in ads may attract a good deal of attention but may not associate the illustration with the product name.

Major steadman reported that brand name associated with sexual illustrations were less easily recalled than were brand names with non-sexual illustrations in their ads.

Regardless of the media used by an advertiser, the designer should strive for a *continuity of design* that will relate each ad to the preceding one in the series and produce cumulative impression to attain fully the objective of advertising campaign. This task can be accomplished in a number of different ways: the same format may be retained (such as picture caption in print, or song and dance in television) . . . a celebrity or unusual model or character may be employed throughout the series.[26] Nirma Washing Powder's ad was presented with the same song for many years, Onida colour television's ad live in the memories of people as it always used a special character i.e. a ghost to present the ad.

John Caple in *Making Ads Pay*, stated if your attention-getting device tries to appeal to everybody by simply shouting "hey everybody!" you may fail to attract the very people who might be interested in buying your product. Copywriters must not inflate readership or listening or viewing audiences by attracting curiosity seekers at the expense of losing customers.[27] Ad copy is to be made to appeal potential customers. Its aim is not to be talked about or liked by general public but to appeal prospects and turn them into customers. It should focus on the potentials and not on anybody else.

In brief, regardless of specific ad medium, copy is usually more effective if it is simple, containing only one or two key ideas; contains a benefit or idea unique to the brand being advertised; is 'extendible' (can lead to several variations in a campaign), flows naturally and smoothly from beginning to end; is specific, using facts and figures and believable details instead of generalities, . . . one overriding rule for developing copy is to keep the format simple, uncluttered, and straight forward . . . TV commercials with too many scene changes, or scenes that are not well integrated should be avoided.[28]

In present scenario an ad copy can give long lasting benefits if:

1. It follow Government rules, regulations and provisions.
2. It follow ideal code of conduct.
3. It consider educational pattern, living standard, source of income, society and cultural heritage and sex.[29]

Bangar (2000) mentioned essential elements of a good copy which every copy maker must strive to include or inculcate in his copy:

(1) Attention value element,

(2) Suggestive element,

(3) Memorising element,

(4) Conviction element (strong, convincible and believable),

(5) Educative element,

(6) Sentimental element (touchy),

(7) Instinctive element (fear, beauty, profit, etc.),

(8) True fact element;

(9) Ethical values element,

(10) Problem solving elements and

(11) Decency and Sociality element.[30]

Different tests are developed to find the effectiveness of ad copies. Copy testing is divided into two major parts, those tests made before the copy is released on a full-run basis (before or pretests—Consumer jury, Rating scales, Portfolio tests, Psychological tests, Physiological tests, Inquiries, Sales tests, Day-after recall tests) and those tests done after the copy is run (after or post tests—Recall tests and Recognition tests).[31]

Copy testing research has received considerable criticism in terms of low validity and reliability associated with the more common copy-testing measures. One major problem is that most such techniques attempt to measure the effectiveness of an advertising campaign based on a single exposure of one commercial.[32] To evaluate the ad copy multiple exposure test is needed.

ISSUES EMERGED

Perusal of the previous studies and researches revealed the following gaps:

1. Prior research works gazed the effectiveness of ad just by their capacity to arise interest about the product among public. While the overall

purpose of ad is to increase the interest to such a level that the prospect take the action of buying an advertised product. So a decision is made to go a step further and study the effectiveness of ad not only in terms of the interest they arise but also in terms of the sales they contribute.

2. Few kinds of ad copies are tested that too in separation so their comparative effectiveness is not known. This gap will be bridged by the proposed detail research work.
3. There exist a vast difference between the nature, qualities and cost of durable consumer goods and non-durable consumer goods. Consequently their ad copy has to be written and designed differently but no attention to this crucial issues has been given in the studies conducted so far.
4. Previous investigations were mainly conducted in the big and metropolitan cities. The consumers of relatively small cities of Rajasthan have different backgrounds and lifestyle so their view point may be different from those of metropolitan residents. There exist a need to study the effect of ad copy on the consumers of the State of Rajasthan.

LOCATION

Udaipur is a district headquarters. Agents and distributors of various consumer products are here so all the advertised products are easily available. Persons of all walks of life live here. Professionals, businessmen, industrialists, government and private employees, all live here. Besides the local mewaris; persons from Wagad, Marwar, Shekhawati, Mewat, Hadoti also reside here. It represents almost all Rajasthan. Persons from other States also reside at Udaipur. Hence it was considered appropriate to carry out the study at Udaipur.

OBJECTIVES OF THE RESEARCH

It is desirable here to spell out the broad objectives of the study in the light of the work done or already in progress in this field in the country. The main objectives of the study were:

(1) To study the need and the growth of ad copy in present market scenario,

(2) To study which type of ad copy consumers like to read, watch and listen,

(3) To measure the influence of various copies of different medias,

(4) To know what type of message really pushes the consumers to patronize the product,

(5) To analyse the suitability of ad copy for a particulars group of product,

(6) To study the advertising copy that is most effective for durable consumer products and for non-durable consumer products and

(7) To give suitable suggestions in the light of the findings of this investigation so more effective and improved ad can be made by the advertisers and by advertising agencies.

RESEARCH HYPOTHESES

The hypotheses formulated for testing under this study are as follows:

1. "The influence of different ad copy on consumers is not similar".

2. "Same type of ad copy cannot be useful for print and for television media".
3. "For durable consumer goods scientific ad copy and for non-durable consumer goods competitive ad copy are most effective".

RESEARCH METHODOLOGY

Sources of Data Collection

Data for this investigation were collected through the primary and secondary sources. The primary data were collected from the consumers of Udaipur district. While secondary data were collected through periodicals, journals, government reports, past studies, research papers, newspapers, magazmes, corporate reports and persons who may have any information on the subject.

Tools for collection of Data

Primary data were collected through the schedules and by personal interview of consumers.

Sample Design

For this study Udaipur district has been selected for collection of primary data. To study the effect of various types of ad copy, 100 respondents were selected on random basis from Udaipur district. Their views regarding the ads of following four consumer durables were collected through systematically designed schedules:

(1) Mobile Phone,

(2) Motorcycle,

(3) Washing Machine and

(4) Television.

As far as non-durable consumer goods are concerned, facts and data relating to the ads of following four products were collected from the respondents:

(1) Tea,

(2) Hair Oil,

(3) Detergent Powder and

(4) Suiting-Shirting.

Field Work

Field work of the present study was carried out during March 2007 to December 2007.

Tools for Analysis of Data

The data collected from primary and secondary source were analyzed by using appropriate mathematical and statistical tools such as percentage, average, weighted average etc.

Importance of the Study

In this research growth of ads and their contribution into sale were studied in detail so the real assessment of advertising effectiveness was made. From the advertising point of view three media channels namely newspaper, magazine and television were analysed, it revealed their comparative effectiveness. Different ad copies relating to four consumer durables (mobile, motorcycle, washing machine and tv) and four non-durables (tea, hair oil, detergent powder and suiting-shirting) were studied and analysed that revealed which type of ad copies are suitable and most effective for each consumer product. Besides these eight products ad copies relating to other consumer durables and non-durables were also studied and analysed that revealed ad copies which are suitable and most effective for each product category. This research is of immense importance for the advertisers and advertising agencies, by using the research-proven effective ad copy they can really build product image, stimulate demand, create new customers, develop new markets, convince and satisfy customers for repetitive purchases.

REFERENCES

1. United States Department of Commerce, National Business Council for Consumer Affairs, *What does advertising do for the consumers*? 1972, p. 8.
2. Wright, S., John, Warner, S., Daniel, Winter, L., Wills Jr., Zeigler K., and Sherilyn, *Advertising*, Tata McGraw-Hill Publishing Co. Ltd., New Delhi 1981, p. 42.
3. Davar, S. Rustom, Davar, R Sohrab, Davar and RN Nusli: *Salesmanship and Publicity*, Vikas Publishing House Ltd., New Delhi 1998.
4. Burnett, John J.: *Promotion Management*, A.I.T.B.S. Publishers and Distributors, Delhi, 1999, p. 277.
5. Weir, Walter: *On The Writing of Advertising*, McGraw-Hill Book Company, New York 1960, p. 156.
6. Bhatia, R.C. : *Business Organisation and Management*, Ane Books, Delhi 2005, p. 171.
7. Sheth, Jabish N.: Measurement of Advertising Effectiveness-Some Theoretical Considerations, *Journal of Advertising*, 3(1), 1974, pp. 8-11.
8. Lavidge, Robert J. andSteiner Gary A.: A Model for Predictive Measurement of Advertising Effectiveness, *Journal of Marketing*, October 1961, pp. 59-62.
9. Czinkota, Michael R., Kotabe: *Marketing Management*, Vikas Publishing House, 2000, p. 399.
10. Sharma, Bhagwati Prakash and Jain, Rajeev: *Functional Management*, Alka Publications, Ajmer 1998, p. 56-59.

11. Luck, D.J., Wales H.G. and Taylore D.A.: *Marketing Research*, Prentice-Hall, New Jersey, 1970 pp. 14-15.

12. Schwartz, D.J. *Marketing Today*, New York: Harcour Brule Jovanovich, 1973 pp. 304-305.

13. Burton, R. Durkee: *How to Make Advertising Work*, McGraw-Hill Book Co., New York 1967 p. 26.

14. Boyd, H.W. and Westfall, R. : *Marketing Research - Text and Cases*, Richard D. Irwin, Illinois, 1964 p. 26.

15. Sudha, G.S.: *Functional Management*, Raj Publishing House, Jaipur 2000 p. 79.

16. Prasad, L.M., *Principles and Practice of Management*, Sultan Chand and Sons Educational Publishers, New Delhi 1995 pp. 620-621.

17. Basotia, Vijay: *Marketing Management*, Mangal Deep Publications Jaipur, 2001 p. 269.

18. Colley, Russel H.: *Defining Goals for Measured Advertising Results*, Association of National Advertisers, New York 1961.

19. Grey, Matter, *Grey Advertising*, Hasting House Publishers Inc., New York, November 1968 p. 8.

20. Sharma, Sandeep and Kumar, Deepak: *Advertising Planning, Implementation and Control*, Mangal Deep Publications, Jaipur, 2001 p. 97.

21. David, Foster Rus: *The Marriage of Marketing and Technology to Improve Company Performance*, Nation's Business, August 1975 p. 44.

22. Higgins, Denis: *The Ali of Writing Advertising*, Advertising Publications Inc., Chicago 1965 p. 17.

23. *Ibid.*, p. 43.

24. Wain, Wright and Anthony, Charles: *The Television Copywriter*, Communication Arts Books, Hasting House Publishers Inc., New York, 1966 p. 90.

25. Oglivy, David: *In Confession of Advertising Man*, pp. 100-102.

26. Wrights, John, Warner, S. Daniel, Winter L. Wills Jr., Zeigler K. and Sherilyn: *Advertising*, Tata McGraw-Hill Publishing Co. Ltd., 1981 p. 468.

27. Caple, John: *Making Advertisements Pay,* Harper and Row Publishers Incorporated, new York, 1957 pp. 3-4.

28. Aaker, David A., Batra Rajeev, and Myers John G.: *Advertising Management,* Prentice-Hall of India Pvt. Ltd., New Delhi, 1995, p. 376.

29. Sharma, Bhagwati Prakash, Jain, Rajeev and Sharma, Jayant: *International Marketing,* Apex Publishing House, Udaipur 2006 p. 271-272.

30. Bangar, R.S.: *Sales Management,* Printwell Publishers Distributors, Jaipur, 2000 p. 481.

31. Boyd, Harper W. Jr., Westfall Ralph Stasch F. an Stanley: *Marketing Research - Text and Cases,* A.I.T.B.S. Publishers and Distributors Delhi 1999 p. 731-732.

32. Multiple Exposure Test Needed to Evaluate Commercials, *Marketing News,* September 21,1979 p. 13.

2 Ad Copy: Components and Kinds

When a company decides to advertise its product, it performs this task itself or appoints an advertising agency to do the advertising. In both cases the media is selected considering the advertising objectives and advertising budget. Then the ad copy is prepared in which advertising idea is conceived, visualized, developed and expressed in words according to the market need and its effectiveness.

> "Advertising Copy consists of heading, coupon, name and address of advertiser, main part of the advertising message which is in written or told form."
>
> —*Willam J. Stanton*

> "Advertising Copy refers to the reading matter that forms the main text of the advertised product in short or detail and' simple or picturised."
>
> —*Auto Klepner*

> "In broader sense advertising copy includes all elements of printed or broadcasted (announced) messages."
>
> —*Right and Burner*

"Advertisement Copy is used to designate all the various types of written material such as the art work, layout and script that are produced as components of printed or broadcasted ad."

—*Rathor B.S.*[1]

The use of word copy is perhaps unfortunate, since it seems only to refer to print media and, more specifically, to the headline and text of the advertising message. Copy refer to an entire ad, including the verbal message, pictures, colours and dramatizations, whether the ad appears in print, on radio or television, or via some other medium.[2]

—*Boyd, Westfall and Stasch*

Ad Copy is the soul of ad. It is all the written or spoken matter in an ad expressed in words or sentences and figures designed to convey the impressive message to the target consumers.

Before proceeding further, it is important to note that the ad copy is concerned with the following:

(a) What to say in an ad,

(b) What to show in an ad, and

(c) How to say and show it effectively.

In a restricted sense ad copy refers to typewritten material which is to be set in type for printed media or spoken by announcers or personalities for broadcast transmission. So the ad copy is the outcome of the efforts of copywriter who writes the words for an advertising message.

In broad sense the words 'ad copy' includes all elements of advertising message and its presentation, either printed or broadcasted. Thus copy for a newspaper ad includes not only the reading matter-headlines, subheads, picture captions, slogans and body of copy but also pictures, trademarks, borders and other illustrations or visual symbols. Copy for a tv commercial includes not only the words to be spoken by the characters in the script but also the music, sound effects, illustrative material, action and camera cues. An ad copy is the product of collective efforts of copywriters, artists and layout men.

> "Copywriter Study Products from the inside out and from top to bottom. They scrutinize intended audiences (wants and needs, likes and dislikes, media and shopping habits) and the competition in painstaking detail. They read and watch, listen and remember, analyze and experiment until they find the right words to express the theme or concept or idea."[3]

Preparing ad copy is not an easy task. Copywriter must have a broad view, he should look at the product through the eyes of prospects and see it as something they may willingly buy, rather than as something the advertiser must sell.

Charles L. Whitter, former creative Vice-President of one of the largest American Advertising Agencies, suggests the ad makers to use aforementioned checklist:

1. Will the product make the purchaser feel more important?
2. Will the product make the purchaser feel more happier?
3. Will the product make the purchaser feel more comfortable?
4. Will the product make the purchaser feel more prosperous?

5. Will the product make the work easier for the purchaser?
6. Will the product give the purchaser greater security?
7. Will the product make the purchaser more attractive or better liked?
8. Will the product give the purchaser some distinction?
9. Will the product improve, protect, or maintain the purchaser's health?
10. Will the product appeal to the purchaser as a bargain?[4]

The ad should be presented in such a way that the answer of maximum aforesaid questions come in yes.

If an ad does not communicate how a product or service answers the prospect's problem, it is like an automobile with square wheels. It may be beautiful, entrancing, memorable and a triumph of creative skills . . . but it will not function![5]

There are different parts or segments or components of an ad copy. Generally the ad copy contain the components mentioned hereafter, but in few cases the ad copy may not have one or more component. To understand all the components two ads First-Himani Navratan Oil and Second-LG Washing Machine are mainly considered. (See ad 2.1 and 2.2).

COMPONENTS OF AD COPY

Headline

A headline is a group of words or a phrase printed often in capital letters implying that an advertising message appears below it. Generally the headline is placed at the top of ad copy and in few cases it can be seen in the middle of ad copy.

It's First job is to attract the attention of reader or viewer and its second job is to draw their attention towards the text or body copy. Headline suggest to the reader or viewer that there is something interesting that follows which he should read or watch. "Attention of readers/viewers is best achieved by headlines that appeals to the reader's self interest (e.g. by offering free, useful information), are newly, offer new twists on familiar sayings, and/or evoke curiosity (i.e. by asking a quizlike question)."[6]

Headlines may be classified on the basis of content and form.

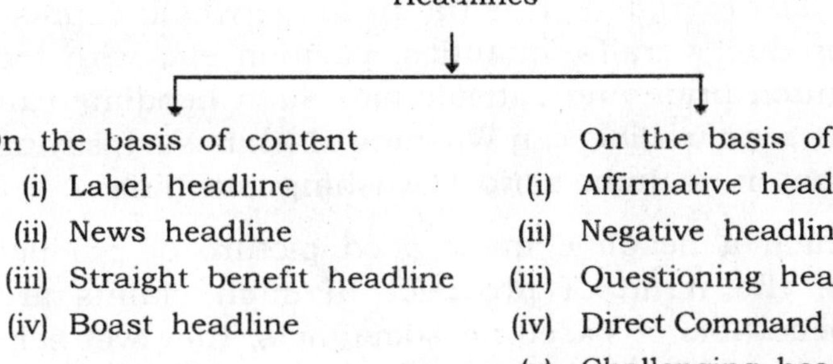

On the Basis of Content

On the basis of content, i.e. the thing which is written or spoken, the headline may be of following kinds:

(i) *Label Headline*—The name of product or Company is used as a headline of ad and nothing else is expressed in headline. To get the attention of viewers directly on the product this can be a good ploy as shown in the ad of 'More' detergent.

(ii) *News Headline*—Any new and fresh information relating to the product may be given as a headline in an ad. The ad of Siyaram-Suitings contains a news headline imparting the information relating to the availability of Siyaram's cloth named Miniature in international style pack.

(iii) *Straight Benefit Headline*—Benefit given by the product is mentioned as a headline. In a straight way the advertiser highlight the product's foremost benefit which a user will have. The headline of LG Washing Machine says "everlasting youth to your precious sarees". In straight way it tells that the machine will take good care of clothes while washing and it is not harsh on them.

(iv) *Boast Headline*—It is the headline which express product's traits, qualities, position etc. with too much pride and satisfaction. Such headline can be seen in Videocon Washing Machines ad, saying that it is India's No.1 washing machine.

Such a headline make good picture of product in the mind of prospect. If such claims are believable or based on some facts, they will help in increasing sales. But they will not do any good if the viewer's find them as sheer exaggeration.

On the Basis of Form

On the basis of form i.e. the particular way in which the headline is arranged and the manner in which it is presented, the headline may be of following kinds:

(i) *Affirmative Headline*—Headline which is expressed in an affirmative manner stating something positively may be called affirmative headline.

(ii) *Negative Headline*—It shows refusal or denial. It generally possess the word no or not. We can better understand this by seeing the ad of Safi. It says "This is not an ad of any face cream, anti-pimple cream, moisturizer or face pack". It implies Safi intrinsically improve the skin and gives natural glow to the face.

(iii) *Questioning Headline*—This headline puts a question before reader or listener e.g. the ad of Himani Navratan Oil at first asks the question" Are you suffering from headache, tension, sleeplessness or hair fall?" The person who is having any of these problems is likely to be attracted with this headline.

(iv) *Direct Command Headline*—This headline authoritatively tells prospects that they must do something. The ad of Onida Colour Television that comes on tv gives a command to the audience to "bring home Onida home theatre".

(v) *Challenging Headline*—Such headline straight way challenges other products on the grounds of design, quality or price.

(vi) *Curiosity Headline*—It raises strong desire among readers to know about the product. Strange and unusual words are also used to raise the curiosity. Its headline is Oh Wow! which means something wonderful but it does not tell what is wonderful. To know that we read the whole ad. Thus curiosity headline is useful, making reader further read the copy.

(vii) *Emotional Headline*—It makes people emotional and tries to take advantage of those emotions. People generally respond very quickly to emotional headline that touches their heart. Magazine ads of Cerelac uses emotional headline. It states my dearest one needs essential nutritional elements in right quantity so I choose Cerelac.

Sub-Headline

This is given below the headline to tell something more about the headline. It enhances the headline making it more clear and understable. In ad of Himani Navratan Oil the sub-headline answers the headline question, saying that the Navratan Oil gives relief from all the problems mentioned in headline.

In ad of LG Washing Machine the sub-headline is 'Unique Fabricare System Washing Machine'. It really gives meaning to the headline. It tells the benefit of longlife for precious sarees mentioned in headline can be achieved with the use of LG Washing Machine.

Slogan

Slogan is made by placing of words or sentences in a rhythmic manner. It not only attracts people's attention but also suggests an idea, very quickly. People easily remember slogans because of their rhythmic nature.

'Thanda Thanda Cool Cool' is the slogan used in ad of Navratan Oil. This slogan is prominently used in TV ad of Navratan Oil.

Just below sub-headline the slogan 'Dirt gone. Clothes go on' is written in the ad of LG Washing Machine.

Illustration

It is used in ad to attract the attention as well as to secure the interest of reader/viewer. The ad of Navratan Oil attracts immediate attention by showing the famous film star Govinda. Govinda is known as 'Hero Number One', and when people see him advertising Navratan Oil their interest develops in watching or reading the ad.

Young naturally beautiful lady with sharp looks and fair complexion grabs the attention of viewers. It suggests if the clothes are washed in LG Fabricare Washing Machine they will remain young and beautiful just like the young lady shown here. Good illustration gives perfect example of product's characteristics, usages, benefits etc.

Body of Copy

It contains the textual type-set-matter which develop the benefit - promise, explain product features and values, and support claims - logically and convincingly. Most of the readers just scan through headline and illustration but the ones with the real buying interest will read the body copy. In other words only the prospects will spend their time to read the details of the product.

The body of LG Washing Machine's ad states that it cleans clothes very gently without harming the fabric and to prove this; three systems of this washing machine namely Punch + 3 pulsator, Turbo drum and Imbalance checker are explained with pictures.

Closing Idea

With attractive illustration and convincing body, desire of having the product is raised but this is not enough. Ad should have a closing idea to persuade the reader or viewer to act: to accept an idea, change an attitude, agree with a proposition, visit a store, ask for a brand name and thereby take a big step towards ultimate purchase of the advertised product. Closing idea may contain any of the following point to persuade the prospects.

(a) Emphasizing convenient accessibility (availability at a nearby location-address)

(b) Providing a coupon

(c) Urging immediate compliance (to take advantage of limited quantities or short-lived sales)

(d) Offering early-bird-shopper specials

(e) Noting easy buying terms (possibly even mail and phone orders with clear addresses and/or telephone numbers included)

(f) Reminding readers of special reasons for buying (birth days, anniversaries)

Prizes worth Rs. 3.5 crores will be distributed among the buyers is the closing idea used to persue the readers to buy the Navratan Oil. Among the prizes the picture of Maruti-800 car, gold jewellery, colour television, suitcases and two-wheeler are shown to motivate the readers. The assurance of gift with every pack of Navaratan Oil is also given.

Information relating to the availability of washing machine in different sizes (in kilograms) and the address of registered office of LG Electronics India Ltd. are given at the end of the LG Washing machine's ad.

Identification Marks

Name of the company, product, its packing, trademark, logo, etc., is give in the ad. People easily memorize them and whenever they go to buy that advertised product, they easily recognize the product and buy it with no hesitation. Hence the advertised mark gives distinct identity to the product.

In the ad of Navratan Oil the bottle of hair oil and its outer cover pack is shown as an identification mark.

In the ad of LG Washing Machine the logo of LG is prominently displayed.

Once all the components or elements of ad copy are conceived and developed, they are systematically put together to form a complete ad. This process of laying out the elements of an ad within specific space limitations is known as layout. In creation of TV ads, the layout is sometimes called storyboard. Like an architect's drawing, the layout for an ad serves as a blueprint.

Generally the ads of different products published in newspapers and magazines and broadcasted on television have great difference in their contents and style of presentation. These ads do not attract or influence us equally. Their designing, pattern, size etc. are different. Actually the advertisers are using different advertising messages and appeals. They are depicting or showing the ad in different types. With the increasing modernisation and competition advertisers really developed following kinds/types of ad copies:

KINDS OF AD COPIES

1. **Straight Selling Copy**—It is the simplest and most common ad copy. It directly says the prospects to buy the advertised product. It is neither tricky nor complicated. It clearly conveys the advertising message to the reader or viewer of Sunsilk hair oil ad published in magazine, is a straight selling ad copy.

2. **Suggestive Copy**—It makes an indirect appeal putting the idea of using the product in the mind of readers or viewers e.g. the tv ad of Saffola edible oil do not directly tells us to buy the Saffola

but it simply suggests that use of Saffola can bring good health. The bulgeing belly, developing obesity and sudden pain of the actor suggests us to be cautious and use low Saffola oil. Life insurance companies also use suggestive copy.

3. **Expository Copy**—It convey the advertising message in clear, understandable and direct manner. It is an open copy that exposes everything about product. Unlike suggestive copy, it is so open that facts are given in very simple and clear way so that there is no need for interpretation. Even for the man or woman of average and below average understanding, a cursory glance is enough to perceive, pick and act.[7]

4. **Descriptive Copy**—The product, its features, qualities and benefits are mentioned in detail. The motive behind it is to give complete information about the product. Prospects can be convinced by giving description of the product from different perspectives. Different mobile phone advertisers are using descriptive copy e.g. the LG mobiles different models' identification numbers, price, picture, different features and the free gift along with each model is givenin ist ad. Besides that various sales points are mentioned.

5. **Poetic Copy**—Ad message is communicated through a poem, rhyme or jingle. Original music or popular film's song is used for presenting ad. The ad of Action School Shoes is a good example of poetic copy it sounds like that "*Classwork. homework, punishment, lecture . . . Good-Good morning teacher . . . Khel . . . Aur ho gai chhutti*".

6. **Scientific Copy**—Scientific data and information relating to the structure, construction and behaviour of the product are given in the scientific ad copy. Such a copy trys to give logical and convincing reasons for buying the product. e.g. the tv ad of Dandi Salt explain the triple refining process that gives highly clean, pure and hygienic salt.

7. **Educational Copy**—It gives knowledge about the product like an educator. It teaches the prospect how to use the product and how it will benefit them. At times it tells additional usages of the product. To some extent the tv ad of Colgate is an educative ad.

8. **Questioning Copy**—Several questions or problems are put before the readers and at last the name of product is mentioned as an answer or solution of all. Nowadays full questioning copy is not used. Only the questioning headlines are used e.g. in the ad of Himani Navratan Oil the following question is asked at the beginning "Are you suffering from headache, tension, sleeplessness or hairfall"? Then the use of Navratan Oil is suggested to get rid of all the problems.

9. **Order Copy**—Hurry up, buy now, make a phone call or fill the coupon and place the order; such hard push tricks are used in this type of ad copy, e.g. the tv ad of tele brands appeal the viewers to send a demand draft of certain amount in favour of tele brands, or make a phone call at the selling points situated in different cities to get the advertised product. The which is very popular bike among youngsters. As per ad Fiero contribution of such an ad in sales can be measured quite easily.

10. **Colloquial Copy**—Ad message is conveyed in informal or local words and phrases, e.g. the villagers chat in local language and suddenly after eating kit-kat they start speaking english all this seems very humorous.

11. **Competitive Copy**—On one or more basis the advertised product is shown better than other similar or substitutable products available in the market. For that purpose comparative graphic or tabular presentation is made.

    The Fiero F2 Motorcycle of TVS is shown better than Bajaj Pulsar in an ad which is very popular bike among youngsters. As per ad Fiero F2 gives more mileage, it has higher power, capacity and pick up.

12. **Institutional Copy**—Instead of emphasizing the product, the position, linage and working of the manufacturing institution are emphasized and highlighted. Reliance Industries Ltd. used institutional ad copy. It suggests Reliance is a socially responsible co. which do not cause any harm to the environment.

    The Haier Electronic uses the institutional copy through this it states it's position in the world and the wide range of home appliances it manufactures. One thing that is noticeable in the ad that not a single products features or qualities are mentioned. Different products of the Haier are shown together to build a grand image of the Haier. Institutional copy is also called Corporate or Image Building Copy. Companies conduct such advertising campaigns to promote the company as a hole and generate a favourable disposition towards the company. Anyone or more of the following points are shown in the institutional copy:

1. Speedy or study growth
2. Fulfillment of social responsibilities
3. Leadership in the field
4. Outstanding performance
5. Long experience and age.

It builds the image of the institution or company. It develops consumer loyalty and extends it from one brand of the co. to another and pave way for a favourable public reception of new products marketed by the co.

13. **Personality Copy**—Famous person or celebrity is engaged to say about the product impressively. The Lux Soap is endorsed by different film actresses namely Karishma Kapoor, Aishwarya Roy, Rani Mukherjee, etc. and even Shahrukh Khan is endorseing Lux. To some extents people start believing that film stars are maintaining or gaining beauty with the usage of lux.

14. **Humorous Copy**—The ad message is presented in an amusing, funny or comic way. The ad message is conveyed in very light and delightful manner e.g. the tv and of Cholrmint and Alpenlebie lolypop are enacted like a joke.

15. **Emotional copy**—It touches the prospect's strong feeling of any kind - love, joy, fear, hate etc. to develop the desire of having the advertised product, e.g. the ad of Saffola edible oil touches our deep emotions and suggests to care for the health of those whom we love and give them the low cholestrol Saffola Oil for their healthy heart and long life.

16. **Exaggeration Copy**—Product's features or effects are exaggerated to mesmerize the prospects. Product is shown as a wonderful and marvelous thing that can completely raise the life of user. For instance the ad of Fair and lovely cream shows that its use can turn a dark lady into a Fair lady within 6 to 8 weeks.

    The stunts shown in the ad of Bajaj Motorcycles cann't be done by any ordinary motorcyclist on the road, these are just exaggeration.

17. **Demonstrative Copy**—The manner of using the product and its effects are depicted in detail so that the prospect can be fully aware of the product. e.g. the tv ad of Vim Bar and Harpik shows that they clean the utensils and the toilet bowls respectively much better than other products.

18. **Testimonial Copy**—Any former user of the product express his or her good experience of using the product. This gives some sort of authenticity to the claim, advertiser is making. In the ad 2.12 Umed Singh Rathor one of the user of TVS Victor express his great confidence in TVS Victor motorcycle. He testify to the Victor's comfort and economy.

19. **Promotional Copy**—Different sales promotion schemes e.g. free gifts, scratch cards, bonus product, discount, finance facility, lower interest rate etc. are prominently shown in the ad to attract and allure the reader or viewer through the ad of Hero Honda is a sheer promotional copy which tells CD Dawn, CD Deluxe and Splendor Plus are available at 0% interest in easy equal monthly installments.

20. **Occasional Copy**—An ad copy which is particularly designed and prepared for a certain festival, anniversary, incident or such other special occasion is called occasional copy. Such an ad copy is not used in normal or routine days. In an ad of Onida Television is drafted particularly for the Janmashtmi i.e. Lord Krishna's birth-day festival. Ad of Samsung electronics is also an occasional ad which announces the discounted price for the marriage season. Both these copies are a mix of occasional and promotional copy.

21. **Drama or Story Copy**—A play or drama or an incident is performed, keeping the product its centre point. The drama raises some curiosity or entertain the viewers to gain their attention. Drama builds a background before saying anything to the prospects.

    Drama copy is generally used with a combination of other ad copies e.g. emotional, humorous, USP, personality copy etc.

    In an ad Motorola mobile phone, an incident where a lady is be fooling one boy and flirting with other boy. All the dramatic incident was caught by Motorola mobile phone and seen clearly through its 2 level Zoom Camera (USP).

    This is a combination of drama, USP and illustrative copy. Drama copy is also known as Narrative copy or Story copy.

22. **Illustrative Copy**—Pictures or photograph take major portion in an ad and very little text message is given. Big illustrations communicate the viewer very clearly and quickly. Besides that people enjoy looking at pictures. Illustrating pretty girls

are popular in advertising. If the girl is truly beautiful, has character and youth's eager interest in life, she is bound to catch and hold attention as sentiments, romance, sex and courage never die.[8]

23. **Elegance Copy**—The advertised product is shown as a superb and graceful thing; that enchants the prospects to such an extent that they start feeling the use of product will increase their position and standard. The ad projects the product as a high class product and much better than the ordinary mass products.

    Raymond uses elegance copy along with the illustrative copy. Man is shown complete and perfect after wearing Raymond clothing. Customers do not buy the product they buy the elegant image of product created by the ad.

24. **Unique Selling Proposition (USP) Copy**—Rosser Reeves, the Vice-President Ted Bates advertising agency originated the USP in early 1940s, when an unique or novel feature/quality of the product is emphasized and claimed to give specific benefit to the prospects in an ad, it is called USP ad Copy for example the tv ad of Anchor White tooth paste claims to be 100% pure vegetarian tooth paste. Pantene claims to stop hair fall up to 94% and it gives enormous strength to the hair, Complain Milk Powder promises to give extra growing power so that children build up quickly, Fevi-quick proposes to stick two surfaces in a moment.

    Such a strong, convincing and saleable attribute or feature is chosen in the USP copy that is only possessed by the advertised brand or not claimed by others even though they may possess.

25. **Child Innocent Copy**—Children have tremendous charm and attraction. They are considered decitless and totally innocent. Nowadays advertisers are using this charm and innocence of children to catch and hold the attraction of readers/viewers. The tv ad of Pears shop and Colgate uses the child innocent copy. In Pears a quite little girl childly chats with her mother. When the daughter see her mother using Pears she asks her "what is it in Pears?" mother replies "nothing". Mother meant in this transparent Pears Soap there is no impurity. Later mother was just telling to herself "what will I wear for going to office". The simpleton girl said "nothing", as she has just listen that particular word, she said that word without knowing its real and pertinent meaning. Mother at first astonished and then smiled at her innocent usage of 'nothing'. She eventually hugged her daughter.

    In Colgate a boy asked teeth related questions to a doctor and doctor calmly answered all his questions and ultimately recommend the use of Colgate toothpaste daily. Which the child and his peer group gleefully accept.

26. **Animated Copy**—When ad message is presented through Cartoons, calcature or other such drawings, it is called animated copy. Clinic Plus Shampoo ad which is presented through animated character. Real looking cartoon films are used to convey ad message on tv. These animated characters are also used along with living performers (human or animal), such ad copy is called semi-animated. Tv ads of Domex toilet cleaner and All Out mosquito repeller are good example of Semi Animated ad copy.

27. **Mixed Copy**—An ad copy which is a combination of two or more type of ad copies is called mixed copy. The ad of Motorola mobile phone is a mixed copy. It is a combination of Drama, USP and Illustrative Copy. Most of the ads today are presented in the mixed form of ad copy.

28. **Full and Original Copy**—The manner and fonn in which the ad is first published or broadcasted giving full knowledge of the product taking large space or time, is called full and original copy.

29. **Truncated and Reminder Copy**—When the original ad is made shorter by cutting off the lesser important things and only the central idea of the original and full-copy is presented, it is called truncated copy. As it only reminds the prospects about the product without giving detailed information it is also called reminder copy.

30. **Tele Based Ad Copy**—When the ad copy used in print media is just a part of ad copy broadcasted on tv and it just reinform or remind about the product, it is called tele based ad copy. Such ad copy is mostly used when the product is widely advertised on tv.

31. **Serial Advertising Copy**—Specific feature of a product is emphasized in the ads over a period of time say 2-3 months. Another feature of product is emphasized or highlighted for the next 2-3 months. In this way different features of the product are emphasized one by one over a long period of time. Ad copy used in this process are called serial ad copy. It has two distinct advantages:

(a) The product remains new in the eyes of public/ prospects and

(b) It satisfy different instincts or needs of the prospects by appealing in different way.

Mobile phone like Nokia is taking good advantage by using this ad copy.

REFERENCES

1. Rathor, B.S., *Advertising Management*, Himalaya Publishing House Bombay, 1995.

2. Boyd, Harper W. Jr., Westfall Ralph, Stasch F. Stanley: *Marketing Research - Text and Cases*, A.I.T.B.S. Publishers and Distributors, Delhi 1999 p. 731-732.

3. Wright, S. John, Warner S. Daniel, Winter L. Wills Jr., Zeigler K. Sherilyn: *Advertising*, Tata McGraw-Hill Publishing Co. Ltd., 1981 p. 397.

4. Whitter, Charles L.: *Creative Advertising*, Holt, Rinehart and Winston Inc., New York 1955 pp. 62-72.

5. Tom, Dillon The Triumph of Creativity Over Communication, *Journal of Advertising*, 4(3), p. 10 Summer 1975

6. Beltramini, Richard F., Blasko Vincent J.: An Analysis of A ward- Winning Advertising Headlines, *Journal of Advertising Research*, April/May 1986 pp. 48-52.

7. Sontakki, C.N.: *Advertising*, Kalyani Publishers, New Delhi 1996 p. 276.

8. Singh D.R. Upadhyay K.M., Tandon R.K., Das N.K., *Advertising With Special Reference to India*, Kalyani Publishers, New Delhi, 1981, p. 91.

3 Ad Copies in Newspaper and Their Effect

People read newspapers to know what is happening all around them. They update their current knowledge with this news reading. As the newspapers contain wide variety of news material namely politics, society, religion, economy, sports, entertainment etc. they serve the interest of different persons having different needs, tastes and instincts. Nowadays newspapers provide all the important local, regional, national and international informations without delay. That's why news reading has become a routine activity of most of the educated persons. To take advantage of this daily habit advertisers publish their products' ad in newspaper. Everyday we can see a number of ad of different product in the leading news papers viz. regional, local and national. They are presented in different manner giving different messages, highlighting different aspects of the product. In nutshell they are using different kinds of ad copy. To understand their distinct effect 100 respondents were selected on random basis and their views regarding ads of consumer durable and non-durable goods were collected through systematically designed schedule by personal interview.

In this book facts, information and data relating to the four non-durable consumer goods namely (i) Tea, (ii) Hair Oil, (iii) Detergent Powder and (iv) Suiting-Shirting are collected. Herein after product wise facts, information, data and their analysis is being presented and written.

TEA

Data relating to tea collected from the schedules are presented in Table 3.1.

Respondents mentioned five tea brands that they have seen in the newspapers. These tea brands mostly used the following kind of ad copy prior to and during the research period. The brief description of these ads is as under—

1. **Brooke Bond Tea**—It uses illustrative copy to advertise its product. The packet of Brooke Bond Taaza tea is prominently shown along with a cup of tea. Besides that three pictures of a lady are shown who works throughout the day and yet remain fresh by drinking Brooke Bond tea. The whole ad message is shown through the pictures using very little words.
2. **Lal Goda Kala Goda Tea**—The ad straight way tell us to buy Lal Goda Kala Goda Tea. Mandira Bedi and another tv artist are shown here totally pleased drinking that tea. The evergreen fragrance of this tea will bring joy on your face. This is a combination of straight selling and personality copy.
3. **Wagh Bakri Tea**—The picture of four glasses and the pack of Wagh Bakri tea are shown in ad. It loudly claims the glasses are free with Wagh Bakri tea. Besides that other ads of Wagh

Bakri claims to give free glass bowls or plastic bucket with each buying of Wagh Bakri tea.

4. **Milap**—The famous Playback singer Nitin Mukesh is shown relishing the Milap tea in the ad. This ad reveals the promotional scheme for the bulk buyers in detail.

5. **Bajaj**—The ad says five exciting prizes can be won by scratching coupon available with Bajaj tea. It allures the readers to buy the Bajaj tea.

All the 100 respondents were requested to fill foue blank spaces with the name of tea whose ad they have seen in newspaper. Thereby 400 names were expected but respondents could mention just 51 names. According to Table 5.1 out of 19 persons who are drinking tea of the mentioned 5 brands just four are such who have not seen any ad in newspapers and still using it and in future out of 22 users just 4 such persons will be there.

In all 15 persons are using and 18 persons will use the tea whose ad they have seen in magazine. It implies that the ads will contribute in future to increase sale by 20%.

As far as these five brands are concerned, newspaper ads are contributing 78.95% to the sale and in future ads will contribute 81.82%. Thus, the effect of ad both at present and in future is extremely positive, they are contributing a lot in sale.

As most of the tea brands are using a combination of two ad copies, it has become necessary to separate these mixed ad copies to find the copy wise effectiveness of each and every ad copy. Hence Table 3.2 is prepared with the help of Table 3.1.

Table 3.1 : Effectiveness of ad copies relating to tea published in newspapers

Sl. No.	Name of Product	Type of ad copy	Persons Saw the ad	Persons liked the ad	Persons saw the ad & using the product	Persons saw & liked the ad and using the product	Persons didn't see the ad but using the product	Persons saw the ad & will use the product	Persons saw & liked the ad and will use the product	Persons didn't see the ad but will use the product
1.	Brook Bond	Illustrative	19	8	3	3	4	4	3	4
2.	Lal Goda Kala Goda	Straight selling & Personality	12	3	2	1	-	3	1	-
3.	Wag Bakri	Promo-tional & Illustrative	9	3	2	1	-	3	1	-
4.	Milap	Persona-lity & promotional	7	2	1	1	-	1	1	-
5.	Bajaj	Promotional	4	1	-	1	-	-	1	-
	Total		51	17	8	7	4	11	7	4

Table 3.2 reveals illustrative, promotional, personality and straight selling copies are seen by 28, 20, 19, 12 persons respectively. In other words they are seen by 35.44%, 25.32%, 24.05% and 15.19% viewers respectively.

Illustrative, promotional, personality and straight selling copies are liked by 44%, 24%, 20% and 12% of the total 25 persons who liked the ad.

As far as copywise effect of ad on sale of tea is concerned illustrative, promotional, personality and straight selling copy stands 1st, 2nd, 3rd and 4th by influencing 9, 6, 5 and 3 persons respectively to use the advertised tea i.e. 39.13%, 26.09%, 21.74% and 13.04% of the total 23 influenced persons.

Almost same trend can be seen in future with a slight increase in the persons who saw the ad and will use the tea.

Here according to Table 3.2 total number of persons are much more than the actual number of persons because the same persons are counted twice or thrice due to the mixed ad copy used by different tea brands.

After study and analysis of Table 3.1 and Table 3.2 it can be said that illustrative copy is the best to advertise tea in a newspaper. It is most seen and liked besides that its influence on usage i.e. sales is highest. On the basis of watching/reminding, liking and usages/ influence promotional, personality and straight selling copy come 2nd, 3rd and 4th respectively.

HAIR OIL

The second non-durable consumer goods that we study is hair oil. Data relating to hair oil collected from the schedules are given in Table 3.3. Respondents

Table 3.2 : Effectiveness of separate ad copy relating to tea published in newspapers

Sl. No.	Types of ad copy	Persons saw the ad	Persons liked the ad	Persons saw the ad and using the product	Persons saw and liked the ad and usinng the product	Persons didn't see the ad but using the product	Persons saw the ad and will use the product	Persons saw & liked the ad & will use the product	Persons didn't see the ad but will use the product
1.	Personality	M7+LI2=19	2+3=5	1+2=3	1+1 =2	0+0=0	1+3=4	1+1=2	0+0=0
2.	Promotional	M7+W9+B4 =20	2+3+1 =6	1+2+0 =3	1+1+1 =3	0+0+0 =0	1+3+0 =4	1+1+1 =3	0+0+0 =0
3.	Straight Selling	L12	3	2	1	0	3	1	0
4.	Illustrative	W9+BB 19=28	3+8=11	2+3=5	1+3=4	0+4=4	3+4=7	1+3=4	0+4=4
	Total	79	25	13	10	4	18	10	4

Here BB=Brooke Bond, L=Lal Goda Kala Goda, W=Wagh Bakri, M=Milap & B =Bajaj mentioned four brands of hair oil that they have seen in newspapers. These four brands mostly used the following kind of ad copy prior to and during the research period. Before discussing their effect it would be better to have a look at their ads published in newspapers.

Himani Navratan

Earlier film hero Govinda, Amitabh Bachchan and later Shahrukh Khan endorsed Himani Navratan oil during the research period. Himani Navratan oil is of very cool nature and it relaxes tensions, headache sleeplessness and stop hair fall and ageing. These unique attributes and specialities are associated with the oil. The description of its composition is given along with the bar diagram to show effectiveness of Navratan oil. This ad as seen in newspapers is a combination of personality, USP and descriptive copy. Maximum number of respondents i.e. 29% have seen this ad.

Bajaj Almond Drops

It always uses illustrative copy as also shown in the ad in newspapers. This ad illustrates a beautiful lady having long thick and stylish hair holding a bottle of Bajaj Almond Drops oil in her hand. The picture of almonds suggests that it is really a natural almond oil and have nothing else.

Shanti Amla

This hair oil has a unique combination of *Amla* and Almond. This novel combination is prominently highlighted. The ad illustrates the bottle of Shanti Amla and an innocent looking youthful lady having beautifully combed thick black hair.

Keo Karpin

The ad tells that Keo Karpin have olive oil too, that keep hair strong and well combed Keo Karpin user lady always looks ready and preety.

Hundred respondents were requested to fill four black spaces with the name of hair oil whose ad they have seen in newspaper. Thereby 400 names were expected but respondents could mention just 67 names. From Table 3.3 we can see that out of 17 persons who are using the hair oil of the mentionedfour brands just 5 are such who have not seen any ad in newspapers and still using it and in future out of 18 users just 6 such persons will be there. In all we see that 12 persons are using the hair oil whose ad they have seen and the same number of persons will also use the hair oil in future.

As far as these four hair oil brands are concerned, newspaper ads are contributing 70.59% to the sale and in future ads will contribute 66.66% to the sale. Thus the effect of ad is very positive, they are contributing a lot in the sale.

As most of the hair oil brands are using a combination of two or more ad copies; it has become essential to separate these mixed ad copies to find the copywise effectiveness of each and every ad copy. Hence Table 3.4 is prepared with the help of Table 3.3.

From Table 3.4 we can see 45 blanks are filled with the name of hair oil that used USP copy to present its ad. After that 38 blanks are filled with name of hair oil that used illustrative copy. 29-29 blanks are filled with name of hair oil that used personality and descriptive copy. In other words they are seen by 31.91%, 26.95%, 20.57% and 20.57% viewers respectively.

Table 3.3 : Effectiveness of ad copies relating to hair oil published in newspapers

Sl. No.	Name of product	Types of ad copy	Persons saw the ad	Persons liked the ad	Persons saw the ad and using the product	Persons saw and liked the ad and usinng the product	Persons didn't see the ad but using the product	Persons saw the ad and will use the product	Persons saw & liked the ad & will use the product	Persons didn't see the ad but will use the product
1	2	3	4	5	6	7	8	9	10	11
1.	Bajaj Almond Drop	Illustrative	22	7	2	2	1	3	2	1
2.	Himani Navratan	Personality, USP and Descriptive	29	7	2	2	-	1	2	-
3.	Keo Karpin	Illustrative and USP	6	2	1	1	3	1	1	3
4.	Shanti Amla	Illustrative and USP	10	3	1	1	1	1	1	2
	Total		67	19	6	6	5	6	6	6

Table 3.4 : Effectiveness of separate ad copy relating to hair oil published in newspaper

Sl. No.	Types of ad copy	Persons saw the ad	Persons liked the ad	Persons saw the ad and using the product	Persons saw and liked the ad and usinng the product	Persons didn't see the ad but using the product	Persons saw the ad and will use the product	Persons saw & liked the ad & will use the product	Persons didn't see the ad but will use the product
1.	Illustrative	B22+K6+S10 = 38	7+2+3 =12	2+1+1 =4	2+1+1 =4	1+3+1 =5	3+1+1 =5	2+1+1 =4	1+3+2 =6
2.	Personality	N 29	7	2	2	0	1	2	0
3.	USP	N29+K6+S10 =45	7+2+3 =12	2+1+1 =4	2+1+1 =4	0+3+1 =4	1+1+1 =3	2+1+1 =4	0+3+2 =5
4.	Descriptive	N 29	7	2	2	0	1	2	0
	Total	141	38	12	12	9	10	12	11

Here B = Bajaj Almond Drops, N = Himani Navratan, K = Keo Karpin, S = Shanti Amla

Both the USP copy and illustrative copy comes at the top with 12 persons liking each copy i.e. 31.58% -31.58% of the total 38 persons who liked ad. Personality and descriptive comes second with 7 persons liking each copy.

As far as the copywise effect of ad on sales is concerned both illustrative copy and USP. copy are at the top by influencing 8-8 persons each to use the hair oil. But in future illustrative copy is a bit better, it will influence nine persons to use the hair oil in future whereas, USP copy will influence seven persons to use the hair oil in future. Personality and descriptive copy are third which influenced four persons to use the hair oil in present and three persons to use the hair oil in future.

Here total number of persons are much more than the actual number of persons because the same persons are counted twice or thrice due to the mixed ad copy used by different hair oil brands.

After study and analysis of Table 3.3 and Table 3.4 it can be concluded that illustrative copy and USP copy are the best to advertise hair oil in newspapers. They are most seen and liked besides that their influence on usage i.e. sales is very high. After them personality copy and descriptive copy are equally effective.

DETERGENT POWDER

The third non-durable consumer goods that we study is detergent powder which is used to clean clothes. Data relating to detergent powder collected from the schedules are given in Table 3.5.

Respondent mentioned three brands of detergent powder that they have seen in newspapers. These three brands mostly used the following kind of ad copy prior

Table 3.5 : Effectiveness of ad copies relating to detergent powder published in newspapers

Sl. No.	Name of pro-duct	Types of ad copy	Persons saw the ad	Persons liked the ad	Persons saw the ad and using the product	Persons saw and liked the ad and usinng the product	Persons didn't see the ad but using the product	Persons saw the ad and will use the product	Persons saw & liked the ad & will use the product	Persons didn't see the ad but will use the product
1	2	3	4	5	6	7	8	9	10	11
1.	Surf	USP and Truncated Copy	31	9	5	4	9	6	4	8
2.	Ghari	Straight Selling and Illustrative	26	12	3	6	2	4	6	1
3.	More	Straight Selling and Illustrative	4	1	-	1	-	-	1	-
	Total		61	22	8	11	11	10	11	9

to and during the research period. The brief description of these ads is as under:

Surf

Surf's ad says that it has a unique low foaming formula with which one can save approximately two bucketful water every day. This ad message is mostly given in truncated form . In other ads of surf the unique strong stain removing formula is emphasised.

Ghari Detergent

Ad 3.10 has a big picture that illustrates, after detailed and painstaking research Ghari detergent is developed. The ad also urges the readers to buy and then believe Gadi's effective cleansing.

More

Ad illustrates the pack of more detergent powder and cake and a smiling lady happy with the clothes cleaned by More. The ad directly and clearly says the readers to purchase More and keep clothes smiling i.e. shining. The ad is presented in a very straight way using no trick or gimmick whatsoever.

All the hundred respondents were requested to fill four blank spaces given in the schedule with the name of detergent powder whose ad they have seen in newspapers. Thereby 400 names were expected but respondents could not mention many product names so the number just stopped at 61.

From Table 3.5 we can see that out of 30 persons who are using the detergent powder of the mentioned three brands just 11 are such who have not seen any ad in newspapers and still using it and in future out of 30 users just 9 such persons will be there. In all we see that 19 persons are using and 21 persons will use the detergent powder whose ad they have seen. It implies that the ads will contribute in future to increase sale by 10.53%.

As far as these three detergent powders are concerned, newspaper ads are contributing 63% to the sale and in future ads will contribute 70% to the sale. Thus the effect of ad is quite positive, they are contributing a lot in the sale.

As all the detergent powders are using a combination of two ad copies, it has become necessary to separate these mixed ad copies to find the copywise effectiveness of each and every ad copy. Hence Table 3.6 is prepared with the help of Table 3.5.

Table 3.6 reveals 31 blanks each are filled with the name of detergent powder that used USP copy and truncated copy. After that 30 blanks each are filled with the name of detergent powder that used straight selling copy and illustrative copy. In other words.

Both the illustrative copy and straight selling copy comes at the top with 13 persons liking each copy. USP copy and truncated copy comes second with 9 persons liking each copy. It shows illustrative copy, straight selling copy, USP and truncated copy are liked by 29.55%, 29.55%, 20.45% and 20.45% of the total 44 persons who liked the ad. Here total number of persons are much more than the actual number of persons because the same persons are counted twice due to the mixed ad copy used by different detergent powders.

As far as the copywise effect of ad on sales is concerned straight selling copy and illustrative copy influence 10 persons in present and 11 persons in future to use detergent powder. USP copy and truncated copy

Table 3.6 : Effectiveness of separate ad copy relating to detergent powder published in Newspapers

Sl. No.	Types of ad copy	Persons saw the ad	Persons liked the ad	Persons saw the ad and using the product	Persons saw and liked the ad and usinng the product	Persons didn't see the ad but using the product	Persons saw the ad and will use the product	Persons saw & liked the ad & will use the product	Persons didn't see the ad but will use the product
1.	USP	S 31	9	5	4	9	6	4	8 2
2.	Truncated	S 31	9	5	4	9	6	4	8
3.	Straight Selling	G26+M4=30	12+1 =13	3+0 =3	6+1=7	2+0=2	4+0=4	6+1=7	1+0=1
4.	Illustrative	G26+M4=30	12+1 =13	3+0 =3	6+1=7	2+0=2	4+0=4	6+1=7	1+0=1
	Total	122	44	16	22	22	20	22	18

Here 5 = Surf, G = Ghari and M = More.

also influenced 9 persons at present and 10 persons in future to use detergent powder. After study and analysis of Table 3.5 and Table 3.6 considering the viewership, liking and influence of usage it can be said that straight selling copy and illustrative copy are the best to advertise detergent powder in newspapers. After them USP copy and truncated copy are equally effective.

SUITING-SHIRTING

The fourth non-durable consumer goods that we study is suiting shirting. Data relating to suiting shirting collected from the schedules are given in Table 3.7.

Respondents mentioned just two brands of suiting-shirting that they have seen in newspapers. These two brands mostly used the following kind of ad copy prior to and during the research period. The brief description of these ads is as follows:

Raymond

The ad illustrates the picture of a man who looks aristocrat in Raymond suit. The brand name Raymond is emphasized and the name of authorised dealers and stockists are mentioned to say prospects where they can get the Raymond suiting-shirtings.

Dinesh

The ad in papres simply puts the list of stores where Dinesh suiting-shirting are sold. The ad illustrates the zoomed picture of a man's upper body that too without face wearing Dinesh suit. The fitting of the suit looks perfect.

All the hundred respondents were requested to fill 4 blank spaces with the name of suiting-shirting whose

Table 3.7 : Effectiveness of ad copies relating to suiting-shirting published in newspapers

Sl. No.	Name of pro-duct	Types of ad copy	Persons saw the ad	Persons liked the ad	Persons saw the ad and using the product	Persons saw and liked the ad and usinng the product	Persons didn't see the ad but using the product	Persons saw the ad and will use the product	Persons saw & liked the ad & will use the product	Persons didn't see the ad but will use the product
1	2	3	4	5	6	7	8	9	10	11
1.	Raymonds	Straight Selling and Illustrative	43	41	5	12	5	6	12	5
2.	Dinesh	Straight Selling and Illustra-tive	12	4	1	1	-	1	1	-
		Total	55	45	6	13	5	7	13	5

ad they have seen in newspaper. Thereby 400 names were expected but respondents could not mention the required number of product names and the number just restricted to 55.

From Table 3.7 we can see that out of 24 persons who are using the suiting-shirting of the mentioned two brands just 5 are such who have not seen any ad in newspapers and still using it and in future out of 25 persons just 5 such persons will be there. In all we see that 19 persons are using the suiting shirting whose ad they have seen. In future 20 such persons will be there that shows a small increase of 5.26%.

As far as these two suiting shirtings are concerned, newspaper ads are contributing 79% to the sale and in future ads will contribute 80% to the sale. Thus the effect of ad is very positive, they are contributing a lot in the sale.

Table 3.7 reveals straight selling copy and illustrative copy are mentioned by the respondents and they are equally effective.

It should not be interpreted in a sense that all the ad copies are equally effective to advertise suiting-shirting in newspapers and any ad copy will be as effective as any other ad copy. It should be understood here that the respondents remember and mention only these two types of ad copies so all the other copies are ineffective in comparison with these two.

To find the composite effectiveness of advertisements relating to tea, hair oil, detergent powder and suiting-shirting Table 3.8 is prepared with the help of the Tables 3.1, 3.3, 3.5 and 3.7.

The analysis of Table 3.9 on the basis of five indicators is discussed below:

Table 3.8 : Composite effectiveness of ads relating to tea, hair oil, detergent powder and suiting-shirting published in newspaper

Particulars	Tea	Hair Oil	Detergent powder	Suiting Shirting	Total
Persons saw the ad	51	67	61	55	234
Persons liked the ad	17	19	22	45	103
Persons saw the ad and using the product	8	6	8	6	28
Persons saw and liked the ad and using the product	7	6	11	13	37
Persons didn't see the ad but using the product	4	5	11	5	25
Persons saw the ad and will use the product	11	6	10	7	34
Persons saw and liked the ad and will use the product	7	6	11	13	37
Persons didn't see the ad but will use the product	4	6	9	5	24

Translation of watching into sale

Out of 234 persons who saw the ads of these four products 65 persons are using these products. That means 27.78% viewers are using the advertised product. In future 71 persons will use these four products out of the 234 persons who saw the ad that means 30.34% viewers will use the advertised product.

Translation of liking into sale

Out of 103 persons who liked the ads published in newspapers 37 persons i.e. 35.92% are using the product. Here the same trend will be seen in future.

Table 3.9 : Effectiveness of separate ad copies relating to tea, hair oil, detergent powder and suiting-shirting published in newspaper

Sl. No.	Types of ad copy	Persons saw the ad	Persons liked the ad	Persons saw the ad and using the product	Persons saw and liked the ad and usinng the product	Persons didn't see the ad but using the product	Persons saw the ad and will use the product	Persons saw & liked the ad & will use the product	Persons didn't see the ad but will use the product
1.	Illustrative	H38+T28+D30 +S55=151	12+11+ 3+45 = 81	4+5+3 +6=18	4+4+7+ 13=28	5+4+2+ 5=16	5+7+4+ 7=23	4+4+7+ 13=28	6+4+1+ 5=16
2.	Personality	H29+T19=48	7+5=12	2+3=5	2+2=4	0+0=0	1+4=5	2+2=4	0+0=0
3.	USP	H45+D31=76	12+9 =21	4+5=9	4+4=8	4+9=13	3+6=9	4+4=8	5+8=13
4.	Descriptive	H 29	7	2	2	0	1	2	0
5.	Promotional	T20	6	3	3	0	4	3	0
6.	Straight Selling	T12+D30+S55 =97	3+13+ 45=61	2+3+6 =11	1+7+13 =21	0+2+5 =7	3+4+7 =14	1+7+13 =21	0+1+5 =6
7.	Truncated	D31	9	5	4	9	6	4	8
	Total	452	197	53	70	45	62	70	43

Here H=hair oil, T=tea, D=detergent powder and S=Suiting-shirting

Translation of sheer watching (excluding liking) into sale

Out of 131 persons who just saw and not liked the ads 28 persons i.e. 21.37% using the products. In future 34 persons i.e. 25.26% of the persons who just saw and not liked the ads will use the products.

Percentage of users who have not seen the ad

Ninety persons are using these four products and out of these 90 persons, 25 are such who have not seen the ad in newspaper. It means 27.78% users have not seen the ad. In future 95 persons will use these four products and out of these 95 persons 24 will be slick who have not seen any ad in newspapers. It means 25.26% future users have not seen the ad.

Contribution of ad into sale

Out of 90 persons who use the product 65 have seen the ad. It means 72.22% users have seen the ads in other words contribution of ads into sale is 72.22%. Out of 95 persons who will use the product 71 have seen the ad. It means 74.74% future users have seen the ad in other words contribution of ads into sale will be 74.74%.

To find the composite effectiveness of every single ad copy published in newspapers relating to tea, hair oil, detergent powder and suiting-shirting Table 3.9 is constructed with the data of Tables 3.2, 3A, 3.6 and 3.7.

Table 3.9 reveals illustrative, straight selling, USP and personality copy are seen by 151, 97, 76 and 48 persons respectively. In other words they are seen by 33.41%, 21.46%, 16.81% and 10.62% viewers respectively. Viewership of other ad copies are much lesser than these four ad copies. Truncated, descriptive and promotional copy are seen by just 6.86%, 6.42% and 4.42% viewers respectively.

Illustrative and straight selling copy are liked by 81 and 61 persons respectively. USP, personality, truncated, descriptive and promotional copy are liked by just 21, 12, 9, 7 and 6 persons respectively. On the basis of liking illustrative and straight selling copy come 1st and 2nd as they are liked by 41.12% and 30.96% of the total 197 persons who liked the ads. USP, personality, truncated, descriptive and promotional copy are liked by just 10.66%, 6.09%, 4.57%, 3.55% and 3.05% of the total persons who liked the ads.

As far as copywise effect of ad on sale of these four non-durable products are concerned illustrative, straight selling, USP, personality, truncated, promotional and descriptive copy influence 46, 32, 17, 9, 9, 6 and 4 persons respectively to use the advertised product i.e. 37.40%, 26.01%, 13.82%, 7.32%, 7.32%, 4.88% and 3.25%, respectively of the total 123 influenced persons. In future illustrative, straight selling, USP, truncated, personality, promotional and descriptive copy will influence 51, 35, 17, 10, 9, 7 and 3 persons respectively to use these four advertised products i.e. 38.64%, 28.51%, 12.88%, 7.58%, 6.82%, 5.30% and 3.27%, respectively of the total 132 influenced persons.

In all we can see a reasonable increase in future in the influence of ads. Considering the viewership, liking and influence on usage it can be concluded that illustrative and straight selling copy stands first and second. After that USP, personality and truncated copy are lesser effective so they stand third, fourth and fifth. Promotional and descriptive copy are just little effective so they stand sixth and seventh.

Information relating to other non-durable consumer goods is also collected it is presented in Table 3.10.

All the hundred respondents were requested to mention four non-durable consumer goods other than tea, hair oil, detergent powder and suiting-shirting whose ad they have seen in newspaper. Thereby 400 names were expected but just 142 names of 31 products were mentioned. Few product ads are presented here to give better' understanding of different ad copies used by them. Out of 142 mentioned names 42 are used. Hence, we can say the translation of watching ad into sale is 29.58%.

As most of the non-durable products are using a combination of two or more ad copies, it has become necessary to separate these mixed ad copies to find copywise effectiveness of each and every ad copy. Hence Table 3.11 is prepared with the help of Table 3.10.

Considering the data of viewership and influence on usage shown in Table 3.12. It is apparent that illustrative copy, straight selling copy and USP copy stands first, second and third respectively. Promotional copy and personality copy seem almost equally effective but promotional copy is a bit better than personality copy. Descriptive copy and truncated copy stands sixth and seventh respectively.

To find the composite effectiveness of each ad copy relating to all consumer non-durables published in newspaper, Table 3.12 is prepared. Comparative effectiveness of each ad copy is judged by the influence it make on the viewers to buy the product. In this process equal weightage is given to both the four products (tea, hair oil, detergent powder and suiting-shirting) and the other non-durable products.

10.21%, 6.82%, 3.73%, 2.02%, 2.10%, 1.61% and 1.06% viewers use the advertised non-durable as they are influenced and stimulated by the illustrative copy, straight selling copy, USP copy, personality copy, promotional copy, truncated copy and descriptive copy respectively. Thus in all 27.55% viewers use the advertised consumer non-durables.

The overall translation of watching ad into sale shown here in Table 3.12 is a bit lower than the actual figures shown in Table 3.8 and Table 3.10. This is because the overall translation of watching ad into sale here is calculated by the summation of influence of each ad copy and in calculation of separate influence of each ad copy the same person may be counted twice or thrice due to the mixed ad copy used by several products.

Illustrative copy is clearly the most effective ad copy followed by straight selling copy and USP copy. Its effectiveness is 49.71% more than straight selling copy and 173.73% more than USP copy. Promotional copy is just a bit better than personality copy. They are 30.43% and 25.47% more effective than truncated copy respectively. Truncated copy is also 51.89% more effective than descriptive, but in totality both are very little effective.

Just like non-durable consumer goods facts, information and data relating to the four durable consumer goods namely

(i) Mobile Phone,

(ii) Motorcycle,

(iii) Washing Machine and

(iv) Television.

are collected through the schedules. Hereinafter product wise facts, information, data and their analysis is being presented and written.

Table 3.10 : Effectiveness of ad copies relating to other consumer non-durables published in newspaper

Sl. No.	Name of Product	Type of ad Copy	No. of persons saw the ad.	No. of persons using the product
1.	Red Chief	Illustrative	4	1
2.	Shakti Bhog Atta	Promotional and Personality	3	-
3.	Ram Dev Spices	Promotional	2	1
4.	Huggies	Straight Selling and Illustrative	6	2
5.	Koutons	Promotional	6	3
6.	ParleG	Straight Selling and Illustrative	7	3
7.	Bhaskar Salt	USP and Straight Selling	11	3
8.	Zandu Balm	USP and Illustrative	3	1
9.	Dabar Anardana	Personality	1	-
10.	Dabar Chyawanprash	Personality	6	1
11.	Campus Shoes	Illustrative	3	1
12.	Himani Fast Relief	Personality and Straight Selling	2	-
13.	Vadilal Ice-cream	Promotional and Illustrative	5	2
14.	Fair and Lovely	Illustrative and USP	9	3
15.	Kayam Churn	Straight Selling and Truncated	6	2

16.	Vasmol	Illustrative and USP	4	-
17.	Jockey	Illustrative	6	2
18.	Himani Sona Chandi Chyawanprash	Personality, USP and Promotional	5	1
19.	Peter England	Straight Selling and Illustrative	2	1
20.	Guruji Squash	Straight Selling and Truncated	3	1
21	Smyle Toothpaste	USP and Promotional	2	-
22.	Colgate Tooth Powder	USP, Descriptive and Illustrative	7	1
23.	Cocal Cola	Illustrative	5	2
24.	Pepsi	Personality and Illustrative	6	2
25.	Thums Up	Strarght Selling	4	1
26.	Saras Milk	Personality and Descriptive	4	1
27.	Action Shoc	Illustrative	4	1
28.	Liberty Footwear	Illustrative	4	2
29.	Philips Tubelight	Illustrative and Descriptive	5	1
30.	Safi	Straight Selling	3	1
31.	Tata Salt	Straight Selling	4	2
	TOTAL		142	42

Table 3.11 : Effectiveness of separate ad copies relating to other consumer non-durables published in newspapers

S. No.	Type of ad copy	Name of Product (number of persons saw the ad/number of persons using the product)	Total number of persons saw the ad	Total number of persons using the product
1.	Illustrative	Red Chief (4/1) Huggies (6/2) ParleG (7/3) Zandu Balm (3/1) Campus Shoes (3/1) Vadilal (5/2) Fair and Lovery (9/3) Vasmol (4/0) Jockey (6/2) Peter England (2/1) Colgate Tooth Powder (7/1) Coca Cola (5/2) Pepsi (6/2) Action Shoe (4/1) Liberty Footwear (4/2) Philips Tubelight (5/1)	80	25
2.	Personality	Shakti Bhog Atta (3/0) Dabar Anardana (1/0) Dabar Chyawanprash (6/1) Himani Fast Relief (2/0) Himani Sona Chandi Chyawanprash (5/1 Pepsi (6/2) Saras Milk (4/1)	27	5
3.	USP	Bhaskar Salt (11/3) Zandu Balm (3/1) Fair and Lovely (9/3) Vasmol (4/0) Himani Sona Chandi Chyawan Prash (5/1) Smyle Toothpaste (2/0) Colgate Tooth Powder (7/1)	41	9

4.	Descriptive	Colgate Tooth Powder (7/1) Saras Milk (4/1) Philips Tubelight (5/1)	16	3
5.	Promotional	Shakti Bhog Atta (3/0) Ramdev Spices (2/1) Koutons (6/3) Vadilal (5/2) Himani Sona Chandi Chyawanprash (5/1) Smyle Toothpaste (2/0)		
6.	Straight Selling	Huggies (6/2) ParleG (7/3) Bhaskar Salt (11/3) Himani Fast Relief (2/0) Kayam Churn (6/2) Peter England (2/1) Guruji Squash (3/1) ThumsUp (4/1) Safi (3/1) Tata Salt (4/2)	48	16
7.	Truncated	Kayam Chur (6/2) Guruji Squash (3/1)	9	3

Table 3.12 : Effectiveness of ad copies relating to all consumer non-durables published in newspapers

Sl. No.	Type of ad copy	Copywise percentage of viewers who said the ad of tea, Hair oil, detergent powder & suiting-shirting*	Copywise translation of watching ad into sale of tea, hair oil, detergent powder & suiting-shirting (in %age)	Ad influenced users of ter, hair oil, detergent powder & suiting-shirting* (3×4/100)	Copywise percentage of veiwers who saw the ad of other consumer non-durables+	Copywise translation of watching ad into sale of other non-durables (in %age)	Ad influenced users of other non-durables (6×7/100)	Average ad influenced users [(5+8)/2]
1	2	3	4	5	6	7	8	9
1.	Illustrative	33.41	30.46	10.18	32.79	31.25	10.25	10.21
2.	Straight Selling	21.46	32.99	7.08	19.67	33.33	6.56	6.82
3.	USP	16.81	22.37	3.76	16.80	21.95	3.69	3.73
4.	Personality	10.62	18.75	1.99	11.06	18.52	2.05	2.02
5.	Promotional	4.42	30	1.33	9.43	30.43	2.87	2.10
6.	Descriptive	6.42	13.79	0.89	6.56	18.75	1.23	1.06
7.	Truncated	6.86	29.03	1.99	3.69	33.33	1.23	1.61
	Total	100		27.22		100	27.88	27.55

* Percentages arc calculated from the data of Table 3.9.

\+ Percentages are calculated from the data of Table 3.11.

MOBILE PHONE (HAND SETS)

Data relating to mobile phones collected through the schedules are presented in the Table 3.13.

Respondents mentioned seven mobile phone brands, that they have seen in newspapers. These brands mostly used following type of ad copy prior to and during the research period. The description of these ads will help us in understanding their analysis.

Nokia

It generally uses promotional and descriptive copy. As we see in the ad four models of Nokia are shown, their identification number, maximum retail price (MRP) and the concessional best huy price are mentioned. Besides that concessional price buyer will get an scratch card on, which one can win different prizes upto Rs. 10 lakhs. Different features of each model are mentioned to give better understanding of mobile's configuration, working and specialities. Sales points are also given at the bottom.

Eight different range of Nokia handsets from Rs. 2,600 to Rs. 36,000 are mentioned along with their model number and MRP are shown in the ad. One thing that is highlighted here is the best buy price which is approximately 10 to 15% lower than the regular MRP.

LG

Just like the ad of Nokia, the ad of LG is presented with promotional and descriptive copy. Another ad of LG describes different features namely recording camera, MP 3, powerful memory, PM, video caller ID etc. of a handset named dynamite 200. It is also available in an exchange scheme at 30% lowered price.

Samsung

Any specific feature of the handset is emphasised and discussed in detail in the ads of Samsung mobile phones e.g. in the an the fliptop feature of Samsung X200 is highlighted and discussed.

Motorola

It generally uses a mix of illustrative, descriptive and personality copy. A picture of five persons is shown in the ad. Their dressing, hairstyle posture and features reflect that they are from entirely different backgrounds having all together different tastes, habit and needs but the Motorola is serving them all. Motorola's different models with their different features and prices cater to the needs of all. The description of different models are give in short and in very specific words in the ads. Film star Abhishek Bachchan endorses Motorola Phones. Here Abhishek is finding joy in dancing on Motorola's PM service.

Panasonic

Very sizzling picture of film actress Bipasha Basu is given in the ads of Panasonic mobiles. Here also one such picture Bipasha is shown in the ad. Different features like colour display, pre-loaded Hindi Hip Tones, internet, MMS and games of Panasonic G60 are mentioned. Several sales points' address and phone numbers are given at the end of ad.

Spice

Just like Panasonic, spice also uses personality and descriptive ad copy to advertise its mobile. Priyanka Chopra endorses Spice mobiles. Different features of each model are mentioned in the ads of spice e.g. in the ad of models S-600 and S-500's features like one touch MP3 player, 128 MB memory, 65k colour display, 64 card polyphonic, loud speaker phone etc. are mentioned. Besides that the ad also says that it is an Indian mobile. Price range and sales and service points are also given in the ad.

Sony

It uses USP and descriptive ad copy in the ad. The low priced colour phones are the USP in the ad. Four model's description is given in this ad. It's ads are some what similar to Samsung's ad.

All the 100 respondents were requested to fill four blank spaces with the name of mobile phone whose ad they have seen in newspaper. Thereby 400 names were expected but respondents could mention just 162 names.

According to Table 3.13 out of 66 persons who are using the mobile phone of the mentioned seven brands just 20 are such who have not seen any ad in newspapers and still using it and in future out of 77 users just 16 such persons will be there.

In all 46 persons are using and 61 will use the mobile phone whose ad they have been. It implies that the ads will contribute in future to increase sale by 32.61%.

As far as these seven brands are concerned, newspaper ads are contributing 69.70% to the sale and in future ads will contribute 79.22%. Thus the effect of ad both at present and in future is very positive, they are contributing a lot in the sale.

As all the mobile brands are using a combination of two or more ad copies, it has become necessary to separate these mixed ad copies to find the copywise effectiveness of each and every ad copy. Hence Table 3.14 is prepared with the help of Table 3.13.

Table 3.14 reveals descriptive, promotional, USP, personality and illustrative copy are seen by 162, 97, 33, 32 and 21 persons respectively. In other words they are seen by 46.96%, 28.12%, 9.57%, 9.27% and 6.08% viewers respectively.

Descriptive, promotional, personality, USP and illustrative copy are liked by 60, 40, 11, 9 and 5 persons respectively. On the basis of liking descriptive, promotional, personality, USP and illustrative copy comes 1st, 2nd, 3rd, 4th and 5th as they are liked by 48%, 32%, 8.80%, 7.20% and 4% of total 125 persons who liked the ads.

As far as copywise effect of ad on sale of mobile is concerned descriptive, promotional, USP, personality and illustrative copies influence 46, 31, 9, 6 and 4 persons respectively to use the advertised mobile i.e. 47.92%, 33.29%, 9.37%, 6.25% and 4.17% of the total 96 influenced persons.

In future descriptive, promotional, USP, personality and illustrative copy also stands first, second, third, fourth and fifth by influencing 61, 40, 11, 10 and 7 persons respectively to use the advertised mobile phone i.e. 47.29%, 31.01%, 8.53%, 7.75% and 5.42% of the total 129 influenced persons.

Almost same trend can be seen in future with a slight increase both in persons who saw the ad and will use the mobile and in persons who liked the ad and will use the mobile.

Here in analysis of Table 3.14 total number of persons are much more than the actual number of persons because the same person is counted twice or thrice due to the mixed ad copy used by different mobile brands.

According to the analysis of Table 3.13 and Table 3.14 it can be said that descriptive copy is the best to advertise mobile in a newspaper. It is most seen and liked besides that its influence on usage i.e. sales is highest. Considering the viewership liking and influence on usage it can be concluded that promotional copy, USP copy, personality copy and illustrative copy stands second, third, fourth and fifth respectively.

MOTOR CYCLE

Data relating to motor cycle collected through the schedules are presented in the Table 3.15. Respondents mentioned five motor cycle brands, that they have seen in newspapers. These brands mostly used following kind of ad copy prior to and during the research period. Description of these ads will help us in understanding their analysis.

Hero Honda

The ad in papers of Hero Honda shows thattwo gram gold ring will be given along with each motorcycle. Besides that 3000 lucky buyers will get four gram gold ring and 300 luck buyers will get 100 gm gold. Another promotional scheme of Hero Honda can be seen in ad 3.48 which states that Hero Honda's different models are available in instalments of Rs. 1,001 at very low interest rate.

Besides that Hero Honda time to time give full page illustrative ads of Karizma, Glamour, Ambition, CBZ and Super Splendor.

Table 3.13 : Effectiveness of ad copies relating to mobile phone published in newspapers

Sl. No.	Name of product	Type of ad copy	Persons saw the ad	Persons liked the ad	Persons saw the ad & using the product	Persons saw & liked the ad & using the product	Persons didn't see the ad but using the product	Persons saw the ad & will use the product	Persons saw & liked the ad & will use the product	Persons didn't see the ad but will use the the
1.	Nokia	Promo-tional & Descrip-tive Copy	65	27	7	17	11	11	20	8
2.	LG	Promo-tional & Descrip-tive Copy	32	13	-	7	3	2	7	2
3.	Samsung	USP and Descrip-tive Copy	30	9	4	4	5	5	5	4
4.	Motorola	Illustra-tive, Per-sonality & Descript-ive copy	21	5	-	4	1	3	4	2

5.	Panasonic	Personality and Descriptive copy	7	3	-	1	-	-	1	-
6.	Spice	Personal lity and Descriptive copy	4	3						
7.	Sony	USP Descriptive copy	3	-	-	1	-	-	1	-
	Total		162	60	11	35	20	22	39	16

Table 3.14 : Effectiveness of separate ad copies relating to mobile published in newspapers

Sl. No.	Types of ad copy	Persons saw the ad	Persons liked the ad	Persons saw the ad and using the product	Persons saw and liked the ad and usinng the product	Persons didn't see the ad but using the product	Persons saw the ad and will use the product	Persons saw & liked the ad & will use the product	Persons didn't see the ad but will use the product
1.	Descriptive	All seven 162 brands	60	11	35	20	22	39	16
2.	Promotional	N65+LG32 =97	27+13 =40	7+0=7	17+7 =24	11+3 =14	11+2 =13	20+7 =27	8+2=10
3.	USP	S30+SO3=33	9+0=9	4+0=4	4+1=5	5+0=5	5+0=5	5+1=6	4+0=4
4.	Personality	M21+P7+SP4 =32	5+3+3 =11	0+0+0 =0	4+1+1 =6	1+0+0 =1	3+0+1 =4	4+1+1 =6	2+0+0 =2
5.	Illustrative	M21	5	0	4	1	3	4	2
	Total	345	125	22	74	41	47	82	34

Here N = Nokia, S = Samsung, M = Motorola, P = Panasonic, SP = Spice and SO = Sony.

Table 3.15 : Effectiveness of ad copies relating to motorcycle published in newspapers

Sl. No.	Name of product	Type of ad copy	Persons saw the ad	Persons liked the ad	Persons saw the ad & using the product	Persons saw & liked the ad & using the product	Persons didn't see the ad but using the product	Persons saw the ad & will use the product	Persons saw & liked the ad & will use the product	Persons didn't see the ad but will use the the
1.	Hero Honda	Promotion and Illustrative	91	35	7	21	-	9	22	-
2.	Bajaj	USP and Descriptive	70	28	5	12	-	6	15	1
3.	TVS	Persona-lity and Promotional	56	17	4	7	1	3	7	-
4.	Yamaha	Promotional and Descriptive	27	8	1	3	-	2	3	-
5.	LML	Competitive and Descriptive	8	3	-	2	-	-	-	-
		Total	252	91	17	45	1	20	47	1

Bajaj

As we see ad, 101 km/l average giving motor-cycle at a very low price nearly Rs. 32,000 is the USP given in the ad. Besides that the description of bike's power, style and warranty is given. Amid rising petrol prices this bike is a real jackpot. Other ads of Bajaj bikes namely Bajaj Platinam, Discover DTSi presents the USP of spring in spring shockers for jerk free ride, alloy wheel for more beauty and power and price nearly Rs. 35,000.

TVS

It uses promotional copy to advertise bikes e.g. in it is stated that gold chain is free with every TVS Victor. Ad shows that it is available at 0% interest or in monthly instalments of Rs. 999 only. India's best cricket player Sachin Tendulkar is shown along with the TVS Victor suggesting that best and leading persons ride this motorcycle. In the ad of TVS Star rising cricket star Mahendra Singh Dhoni is shown.

Yamaha

Different promotional schemes are highlighted in Yamaha's ads. In the ad, we see that the insurance is free on purchase of Yamaha bikes, besides that there is a discount of Rs. 2,000 on Yamaha Libero. Description of both bikes are given just below their picture from which one can understand the capacity and performance of each bike. Ad 3.52 highlights another promotional scheme in which two full tank petrol is free on purchase of Yamaya. The description of each bike is also given in the ad.

LML

LML generally uses competitive and descriptive ad copy to advertise its motorcycles. As we see in the ad the LML freedom is shown better than Hero Honda's Passion and Pas-sion Plus. The ad boastly states that BBC (British Broadcasting Corporation) has declared LML Freedom is India's best bike. To substantiate the claim comparison on the basis of engine capacity and power is made among LML Freedom, Passion Plus and Passion. To describe the bike's qualities its average, price, balance, style and control are mentioned in the ad.

During research all the hundred respondents were requested to fill four blank spaces with the name of motorcycle whose ad they have seen in newspaper. Thereby 400 names were expected but respondents mention just 252 names.

According to Table 3.15 out of 63 persons who are using the motorcycle of the mentioned five brands merely one person is there who have not seen any ad in newspapers and still using it and in future out of 65 users just one will be there who use motor cycle without even seeing an ad in newspaper.

In all 62 persons are using and 67 persons will use the motorcycle whose ad they have seen. It implies that the ads will contribute in future to increase sale by 8.06%.

As far as these five brands are concerned, newspaper ads are contributing 98.41% to the sale and in future ads will contribute 98.53%. Thus the effect of ad both at present and in future is extremely positive; they are contributing almost 100% in the sale.

As all the motorcycle brands are using a combination

of two ad copies; it has become essential to separate these mixed ad copies to find the copy wise effectiveness of each and every ad copy. Hence Table 3.16 is prepared with the data of Table 3.15.

Table 3.16 reveals promotional, descriptive, illustrative, USP personality and competitive copy are seen by 174, 105, 91, 70, 56 and 8 persons respectively. In other words they are seen by 34.52% 20.83%, 18.06%, 13.89%, 11.11% and 1.59% veiwers respectively. Promotional, descriptive, illustrative, USP, personality competitive copy are liked by 60, 39, 35, 28, 17 and 3 person respectively. On the basis of liking promotional, descriptive, illustrative, USP and personality copy come 1st, 2nd, 3rd, 4th and 5th as they are liked by 32.97%, 21.43%, 19.23%, 15.38% and 9.34% of total 182 persons who liked the ad competitive copy is at the bottom as it is liked by merely 1.65% of the total persons.

As far as copywise effect of ad on sale of motorcycle is concerned promotional, illustrative, descriptive, USP, personality and competitive copies influence 43, 28, 23, 17, 11 and two persons respectively to use the advertised motorcycle i.e. 34.68%, 22.58%, 18.55%, 13.71%, 8.87% and 1.61% of the total 124 influenced persons.

In future promotional, illustrative, descriptive, USP and personality copies will influence 46, 31, 26, 21 and 10 persons respectively to use the advertised motorcycle i.e. 34.33%, 23.14%, 19.40%, 15.67% and 7.46% of the total 134 influenced persons.

We can easily find a reasonable increase in the persons who saw the ad and will use the motorcycle and the persons who liked the ad and will use the motorcycle as compared to the present with an exception

Table 3.16 : Effectiveness of separate ad copies relating to motorcycle published in newspapers

Sl. No.	Types of ad copy	Persons saw the ad	Persons liked the ad	Persons saw the ad and using the product	Persons saw and liked the ad and usinng the product	Persons didn't see the ad but using the product	Persons saw the ad and will use the product	Persons saw & liked the ad & will use the product	Persons didn't see the ad but will use the product
1.	Promotional	H91+T56+Y27 =174	35+17+ 8=60	7+4+1 =12	21+7+3 =31	0+1+0 =1	9+3+2 =14	22+7+3 =32	0+0+0 =0
2.	Illustrative	H91	35	7	21	0	9	22	0
3.	Descriptive	B70+Y27+L8 =105	28+8+3 =39	5+1+0 =6	12+3+2 =17	0+0+0 =0	6+2+0 =8	15+3+0 =18	1+0+0 =1
4.	USP	B70	28	5	12	0	6	15	1
5.	Personality	T56	17	4	7	1	3	7	0
6.	Competitive	L8	3	0	2	0	0	0	0
	Total	504	182	34	90	2	40	94	2

Here H=Hero Honda, B=Bajaj, T=TVS, Y=Yamaha and L=LML

of competitive ad copy that will not influence anyone in future to use the motorcycle.

Here in analysis of Table 3.16 total number of persons are much more than the actual number of persons because the same person is counted twice or thrice due to the mixed ad copy used by different motorcycle brands.

After study and analysis of Table 3.15 and Table 3.16 it can be said that promotional copy is the best to advertise motorcycle in a newspaper. It is most seen and liked besides that its influence on usage i.e. sales is highest. Considering the viewership, liking and influence on usage it can be concluded that illustrative copy, descriptive copy, USP copy and personality copy stands second, third, fourth and fifth respectively. While the effectiveness of competitive copy is trivial.

WASHING MACHINES

Data relating to washing machines collected through the schedules are presented in Table 3.17 respondents mentioned eight washing machine brands, that they have seen in newspapers. These brands mostly used following kind of ad copy prior to and during the research period. Description of these ads will help is in understanding their analysis better.

Videocon

Pictures of four models of Videocon Washing Machine are illustrated in Ad 2.5. Besides that their lower prices are highlighted. In the ad the pictures of semi-automatic washing machine and free Cello bath set given under *har din diwali* promotional offer are illustrated. Videocon generally uses illustrative and promotional copy.

LG

It uses promotional and descriptive ad copy. As we can see in the ad one thousand rupees special deduction on semi-automatic washing machine is prominently shown. Besides that the salient features of washing machine are mentioned namely easy drainer, extra large capacity, hot and cold water inlet and collar scrubber.

Whirlpool

1-2, 1-2 hand wash system is the USP given in the ads of Whirlpool. As we see the ad various reasons of easy cleansing with Whirlpool washing machine are given. It has aqua shower, unimix detergent dispcnser, soak option, three wash programmes, see through window, wheel castor, 340 watts motor and heater option.

Samsung

Pictures of different washing machines of Samsung are illustrated in newspapers can be seen. Time to time different promotional schemes are introduced and advertised a card game of heart matching is highlighted through which one can win 126 exciting prizes like Santro Xing Car, Samsung refrigerate Singer Blender, Samsung Microwave Oven, etc.

Maharaja Whiteline

It uses promotional and descriptive copy. Novel exchange offer in which reduction of rupees two thousand will be given for the old refrigerate, colour tv, music system, washing machine, VCR or VCP purchase of Maharaja Whiteline Washing Machine. The description of washing machines' functioning is also given in the adsin newspapers.

Table 3.17 : Effectiveness of ad copies relating to washing machine published in newspapers

Sl. No.	Name of product	Type of ad copy	Persons saw the ad	Persons liked the ad	Persons saw the ad & using the product	Persons saw & liked the ad & using the product	Persons didn't see the ad but using the product	Persons saw the ad & will use the product	Persons saw & liked the ad & will use the product	Persons didn't see the ad but will use the the
1.	Videocon	Promotional and Illustrative	43	17	3	5	3	5	8	2
2.	LG	Descriptive and Promotional	35	12	2	4	1	3	4	1
3.	Whirlpool	USP and Descriptive	38	10	3	5	-	4	5	1
4.	Samsung	Illustritive and Promotional	30	8	1	3	-	2	3	
5.	Maharaja	Promotional and Descriptive	7	2	-	1	1	-	1	1

6.	Godrej	Personality, USP and Promotional	8	3	-	1	-	2	1	
7.	Oinda	Promotional and USP	22	6	3	2	1	4	2	2
8.	Electrolux Kelvinator	Promotional and Descriptive	5	1	-	1	-	-	1	-
	Total		188	59	12	22	6	20	25	7

Godrej

It uses a combination of personality, USP an promotional ad copy. The famous lively film actress Preet Zinta endorses Godrej Washing Machine. These machines throw water with pressure from all four sides so every dirt particle is released from the cloth. This USP is presented in short as four side power washing machine. As we see in ad, special price reduction is offered on all four models of washing machine.

Onida

400 Watt powerful motor is the USP presented in the ads of Onida Washing Machine. Besides that one or another promotional scheme is given in the ad to attract the prospect. There are three promotional attractions first scratch and win offer with a certain price second lower price and third 0% finance facility.

Electrolux Kelvinator

It uses promotional and descriptive ad copy. Two promotional attractions are highlightedin the ads. First one thousand rupees special reduction in price and second the machine is available at 0% interest in ten easy instalments of Rs. 699 each.

Salient features of the machine are mentioned namely, turbo wash, 350 watt motor, turbo rinse, dirt expeller brush, active soak brush, 6 kg capacity.

During research all the 100 respondents were requested to fill four blank spaces with the name of washing machine whose ad they have seen in newspapers. Thereby 400 names were expected but respondents mention just 188 names.

According to Table 3.17 out of 40 persons who are using the washing machine of the mentioned eight brands just 6 are such who have not seen any ad in newspapers and still using it and in future out of 52 users just 7 such persons will be there.

In all 34 persons are using and 45 persons will use the washing machine whose ad they have seen. It implies that the ads will contribute in future to increase sale by 32.35%.

As far as these eight brands are concerned newspapers ads are contributing 85% to the sale and III future ads will contribute 86.54%. Thus the effect of ad both at present and in future is highly positive, they are contributing a lot in the sales.

As all the washing machines are using a combination of two or more ad copies, it has become essential to separate these mixed ad copies to find the copywise effectiveness of each and every ad copy. Hence Table 3.18 is prepared with the help of Table 3.17.

Table 3.18 reveals promotional, descriptive, illustrative and USP copy are seen by 150, 85, 77 and 68 persons respectively. In other words they are seen by 38.66%, 21.91%, 19.84% and 17.53% viewers respectively. Personality copy is seen by merely 2.06% veiwers.

Promotional, descriptive, illustrative, USP and personality copy are liked by 49, 25, 25, 19 and 3 persons respectively. On the basis of liking promotional copy is at the top as it is liked by 40.50% persons who liked the ads. Descriptive and illustrative copy jointly stands second, they are liked by 20.66%-20.66% of the total 121 persons who likes the ad. USP copy comes third as it is liked by 15.70% of the total 121 persons who liked the ad. Personality copy is at the bottom as

Table 3.18 : Effectiveness of separate ad copies relating to washing machine in newspapers

Sl. No.	Types of ad copy	Persons saw the ad	Persons liked the ad	Persons saw the ad and using the product	Persons saw and liked the ad and usinng the product	Persons didn't see the ad but using the product	Persons saw the ad and will use the product	Persons saw & liked the ad & will use the product	Persons didn't see the ad but will use the product
1.	Promotional	V43+LG35 +S30+M7 +08+On22 +E5=150	17+12+ 8+2+3+ 6+1=49	3+2+1 +0+0+ 3+0=9	5+4+3+ 1+1+2+ 1=17	3+1+0+ 1+0+1 + 0=6	5+3+2+ 0+2+4+ 0=16	8+4+3+ 1+1+2+ 1=20	2+1+0+ 1+0+2+ 0=6
2.	Descriptive	LG35+W38 +M7+E5=85	12+10+ 2+1=25	2+3+0 +0=5	4+5+1+ 1=11	1 +0+1+ 0=2	3+4+0+ 0=7	4+5+1+ 1=11	1+1+1+ 0=3
3.	Illustrative	V43+S30=77	17+8 =25	3+1=4	5+3=8	3+0=3	5+2=7	8+3=11	2+0=2
4.	USP	W38+G8 +On22=68	10+3+6 =19	3+0+3 =6	5+1+2 =8	0+0+1 =1	4+2+4 =10	5+1+2 =8	1+0+2 =3
5.	Personality	G8	3	0	1	0	2	1	0
	Total	388	121	24	45	12	42	51	14

Here V=Videocon, W=Whirlpool, S=Samsung, M=Maharaja Whiteline, G=Godrej, On=Onida and E=Electrolux Kelvinator it is liked by merely 2.48% persons who liked the ads.

As far as copywise effect of ad on sale of washing machine is concerned promotional, descriptive, USP, illustrative and personality copy stands 1st, 2nd, 3rd, 4th and 5th respectively by influencing 26, 16, 14, 12 and 1 person respectively to use the advertised washing machine i.e. 37.68%, 23.19%, 20.29%, 17.39% and 1.45% of the total 69 influenced persons.

In future also promotional copy will be at top by influencing 36 persons i.e. 38.71% of the total 93 influenced persons. Descriptive, USP and illustrative copy jointly come second as they will influence 18 persons each i.e. 19.35%-19.35% of the total influenced persons. Personality copy is third by influencing 3 persons i.e. 3.24% of the total influenced persons. We can easily find a good increase in future in the persons who saw the ad and will use the washing machine and the persons who liked the ad and will use the washing machine as compared to the present.

Here in analysis of Table 3.18 total number of persons are much more than the actual number of persons because the same person is counted twice or thrice due to the mixed ad copy used by different washing machine brands.

According to the analysis of Table 3.17 and Table 3.18 it can be said that promotional copy is the best to advertise washing machine in a newspaper. It is most seen and liked besides that its influence on usage i.e. sales is highest.

Considering the viewership, liking and influence on usage it can be concluded that descriptive copy, illustrative copy, USP copy and personality copy stands second, third, fourth and fifth respectively.

TELEVISION

Data relating to television sets collected through the schedules are presented in Table 3.19. Respondents mentioned eight television brands, that they have seen in newspapers. These brands mostly used following kind of ad copy prior to and during the research period. Description of these ads will help in understanding their analysis better.

Videocon

One of the best film actors Shahrukh Khan endorses Videocon. Different models of different sizes of Videocon TV sets are illustrated. This combination of personality and illustrative copy is frequently published in newspapers.

LG

LG generally advertise different promotional schemes. The novel exchange scheme is highlighted in the ad, which one can get LG Flatron and a DVD Player in exchange of any old colour tv for just Rs. 9,990. Key features of the tv and details of promotional schemes are mentioned.

Another promotional scheme is highlighted in ad in newspapers. On purchase of LG TV+LG GSM Mobile one can get an advantage of saving Rs. 3,000 to Rs. 4,000. Scratch and win offer is also advertised time to time.

Samsung

Pictures of different models are illustrated in the ads of Samsung TV. This we can see in Ad 3.66.

Television sets of 53 and 74 cm screen sizes are shown, along with their exchange prices. Three promotional incentives are given in the ad first old tv can be replaced/ exchanged with new Sumsung TV for just Rs. 5,000 to Rs. 12,000, second finance at 0% interest rate and third no processing fees.

Besides that big picture of Samsung LCD TV is illustrated in one fourth page of newspaper.

Onida

The picture of a monster is frequently illustrated in the ads of Onida TV. A comparison of Onida TV with LG and Samsung TV is shown in the ad. In the comparison Onida is shown more advanced and technically modem. It has digital eye, surround sound, music mode, front AV and zap features which LG and Samsung do not have.

Onida also uses promotional schemes in ads, three promotional incentives are given. First scratch and win offer, second free headphone and third special festive prices which are quite lower than the MRP. Besides that description of each model is given in the ads. Its special features are mentioned.

Bush

The lower price of Bush TV is presented as a big advantage given by the company to the consumers. By opening its own showroom and cutting the distributors and dealers profit, company managed to provide Bush CTV at a very alluring price. Here in ads the promotional message is that the Bush TV is available to the consumers at factory price.

Table 3.19 : Effective of ad copies relating to television published in newspapers

Sl. No.	Name of pro-duct	Types of ad copy	Persons saw the ad	Persons liked the ad	Persons saw the ad and using the product	Persons saw and liked the ad and usinng the product	Persons didn't see the ad but using the product	Persons saw the ad and will use the product	Persons saw & liked the ad & will use the product	Persons didn't see the ad but will use the product
1	2	3	4	5	6	7	8	9	10	11
1.	Videocon	Persona-lity and Illustrative	57	22	5	12	3	5	13	3
2.	LG	Promo-tional and Descriptive	36	13	3	8	4	5	9	3
3.	Samsung	Illustritive and Promotional	30	7	3	3	1	3	3	1
4.	Onida	Promo-tional,	22	6	1	1	2	1	2	1

	Illustrative, Descriptive and Competitive								
5. Bush	Promotional	12	3	-	2	1	1	2	1
6. Sansui	USP and Descriptive	5	2	-	1	-	1	1	-
7. Sony	Promotional and Descriptive	10	2	1	1	-	2	1	-
8. Akai	Promotional and Descriptive	12	3	2	2	1	3	2	1
	Total	184	58	IS	30	12	21	33	10

Sansui

The powerful rocking 1500 Watt PMPO sound output is the USP highlighted in the ads of Sansui TV. Sansui is named as Hard Rock TV. Besides that different other features are mentioned in the ads of Sansui TV which we can see in adsin newspapers.

Sony

It uses promotional copy in the ads, zero per cent finance and low EMI is highlighted to attract the readers. Salient features of the TV are also mentioned to give better understanding of the product to the prospects.

Akai

Akai also uses promotional and descriptive copy. Two promotional schemes namely exchange offer and 0% finance are prominently showedin newspapers. Akai generally motivate people to exchange their old tv with new large 74 cm tv. Brief description of different models are also shown in newspapers.

During research all the hundred respondents were requested to fill four blank spaces with the name of tv whose ad they have seen in newspaper. Thereby 400 names were expected but respondents mention just 184 names.

According to Table 3.19 out of 57 persons who are using the tv of the mentioned eight brands just 12 are such who have not seen any ad in newspapers and still using it and in future out of 64 users just 10 such persons will be there.

In all 45 persons are using and 54 persons will use the tv whose ad they have seen. It implies that the ads will contribute in future to increase sale by 20%.

As far as these eight brands are concerned, newspaper ads are contributing 78.95% to the sale and in future ads will contribute 84.38%. Thus the effect of ad both at present and in future is highly positive, they are contributing a lot in the sales.

As all the televisions are using a combination of two or more ad copies, it has become essential to separate these mixed ad copies to find the copy wise effectiveness of each and every ad copy. Hence Table 3.20 is prepared with the help of Table 3.19.

From Table 3.20 we can see 122 blanks are filled with the name of televisions that used promotional copy to present its ad. After that 109, 85, 57 and 22 persons have seen the ad of TVs that used illustrative, descriptive, personality and competitive copy respectively. USP copy is at the bottom with just 5 persons saw it. In other words they are seen by 30.50%, 27.25%, 21.25%, 14.25%, 5.50% and 1.25% viewers respectively.

Illustrative, promotional, descriptive, personality, competitive and USP copy are liked by 35, 34, 26, 22, 6 and two persons respectively. On the basis of liking illustrative, promotional, descriptive and personality copy come 1st, 2nd, 3rd and 4th as they are liked by 28%, 27.20%, 20.80% and 17.60% of the total 125 persons who liked the ads. competitive and USP copy come 5th and 6th as they are liked by merely 4.80% and 1.60% of total persons who liked ads.

As far as copywise effect of ad on sale of tv is concerned promotional, illustrative, descriptive, personality, competitive and USP copy influence 27, 25, 20, 17, 2 and 1 person respectively to use the advertised tv i.e. 29.35%, 27.17%, 21.74%,18.48%, 2.17% and 1.09% of the total 92 influenced persons.

Table 3.20 : Effectiveness of separate ad copies relating to TV published in newspapers

Sl. No.	Types of ad copy	Persons saw the ad	Persons liked the ad	Persons saw the ad and using the product	Persons saw and liked the ad and usinng the product	Persons didn't see the ad but using the product	Persons saw the ad and will use the product	Persons saw & liked the ad & will use the product	Persons didn't see the ad but will use the product
1.	Promotional	LG36+ On22+B12 +Sy10+A12 +S30=122	13+6+3 +2+3+7 =34	3+1+0 +1+2+ 3=10	8+1+2+ 1+2+3 =17	4+2+1+ 0+1+1 =9	5+1+1+ 2+3+3= 15	9+2+2+ 1+2+3 =19	3+1+1+ 0+1+1 =7
2.	Illustrative	V57+S30+ On22 =109	22+7+6 =35	5+3+1 =9	12+3+1 =16	3+1+2 =6	5+3+1 =9	13+3+2 =18	3+1+1 =5
3.	Descriptive	LG36+On22 +Si5+Sy10 +A12=85	13+6+2 +2+3 =26	3+1+0 +1+2 =7	8+1+1+ 1+2 =13	4+2+0+ 0+1 =7	5+1+1+ 2+3 =12	9+2+1+3+ 1+2 =15	1+0+ 0+1 =5
4.	Personality	V57	22	5	12	3	5	13	3
5.	Competitive	On22	6	1	1	2	1	2	1
6.	USP	Si5	2	0	1	0	1	1	0
	Total	400	125	32	60	27	43	68	21

Here V=Videocon, S=Samsung, On=Onida, B=Bush, Si=Sansui, Sy= Sony and A=Akai

In future also promotional copy is at the top by influencing 34 persons i.e. 30.64% of the total 111 influenced persons. Illustrative and descriptive copy are equally effective by influencing 27 persons each i.e. 24.32%-24.32% of the total influenced persons. Personality, competitive and USP copy influenced 18, 3 and 2 persons respectively to use advertised tv i.e. 16.22%, 2.70% and 1.80% of the total 111 influenced persons.

It shows a reasonable increase in future in the persons who saw the ad and will use the tv and the persons who liked the ad and will use the tv as compared to the present.

Here in analysis of Table 3.20 total number of persons are much more than the actual number of persons because the same person is counted more than oncc duc to the mixed ad copy used by different television brands.

According to the analysis of Table 3.19 and Table 3.20 it can be said that promotional copy is the best to advertise tv sets in a newspaper. It is most seen and highly liked besides that its influence on usage i.e. sales is highest.

Considering the viewership, liking and influence on usage it can be concluded that illustrative copy, descriptive copy, personality copy, competitive copy and USP copy stands second, third, fourth, fifth and sixth respectively to advertise tv sets in newspapers.

To find the composite effectiveness of ads relating to mobile, motor cycle, washing machine and television, Table 3.21 is prepared with the help of Table 3.13, Table 3.15, Table 3.17 and Table 3.19. The analysis of Table 3.21 on the basis of five points is discussed below :

Table 3.21: Composite effectiveness of ads relating to mobile, motorcycle, washing machine and tv published in newspapers

Particulars	Mobile	Motor-cycle	Washing Machine	TV	Total
Persons saw the ad	162	252	188	184	786
Persons liked the ad	60	91	59	58	268
Persons saw the ad and using the product.	11	17	12	15	55
Persons saw and liked the ad & using the product.	35	45	22	30	132
Persons didn't see the adbut using the product.	20	1	6	12	39
Persons saw the ad and will use the product.	22	20	20	21	83
Persons saw and liked the ad and will use the product.	39	47	25	33	144
Persons did not see the ad but will use the product.	16	1	7	10	34

Translation of watching into sale

Out of 786 persons who saw the ads of these four products 187 persons are using these products, that means 23.79% viewers are using the advertised product. In future 227 persons will use these four products out of 786 persons who saw the ad that means 28.88% viewers will use the advertised product.

Translation of liking into sale

Out of 268 persons who liked the ads published in newspapers 132 persons i.e. 49.25% are using the product. In future 53.73% of the people who liked the ad, will use the product.

Translation of Sheer Watching (excluding liking) into sale

Out of 518 persons who just saw and not liked the ads, 55 persons i.e. 10.62% are using the advertised products. In future 83 persons i.e. 16.02% of the persons who just saw and not liked the ads, will use the products.

Percentage of users who have not seen the ad

226 persons are using these four products, out of these 226 users just 39 persons have not seen the ad in newspaper. It means 17.26% users have not seen the ad.

In future 261 persons will use these four products and out of them just 34 will be such who have not seen the ad in newspaper. It means 13.03% future users have not seen the ad.

Contribution of ad into sale

Out of 226 persons who use the product 187 have seen the ad. It means 82.74% users have seen the ad in other words contribution of ads into sale is 82.74%.

Out of 261 persons who will use the product 227 have see the ad. It means 86.97% future users have seen the ad, in other words contribution of ads into sale will be 86.97%.

To find the composite effectiveness of every single ad copy published in newspapers relating to mobile, motocycle, washing machine and TV. Table 3.22 is prepared with the help of Tables 3.14, 3.16, 3.18 and 3.20.

According to Table 3.22 promotional copy is at the top with 543 persons saw it. Descriptive, illustrative and USP copy stands second, third and fourth with 437, 298 and 176 viewers respectively. Personality and competitive copy stands fifth and sixth as they are seen by 153 and 30 persons respectively. In other words these copies are seen by 33.17%, 26.70%, 18.20%, 10.75%, 9.35% and 1.83% viewers respectively.

Promotional, descriptive, illustrative, USP, personality and competitive copy are liked by 183, 150, 100, 58, 53 and 9 persons respectively. On the basis of liking promotional, descriptive, illustrative, USP and personality copy come 1st, 2nd, 3rd, 4th and 5th as they are liked by 33.09%, 27.13%, 18.08%, 10.49% and 9.58% of the total 553 persons who liked the ads. Competitive copy is liked by merely 1.83% of the total persons who liked the ads.

As far as copywise effect of ad on sale of these four consumer durables are concerned promotional, descriptive, illustrative, USP, personality and competitive copy influence 127, 105, 69, 41, 35 and 4 persons respectively to use the advertised product i.e. 33.33%, 27.56, 18.11%, 10.76%, 9.19% and 1.05% of the total 381 influenced persons.

In future also promotional and descriptive copy come 1st and 2nd by influencing 156 and 132 persons respectively i.e. 33.40% and 28.27% of the total 467 influenced persons. Illustrative, USP and personality copy come 3rd, 4th and 5th as they will influence 83, 52 and 41 persons respectively i.e. 17.77%, 11.14%

and 8.78% of the total influenced person. Competitive copy will influence just three persons i.e. 0.64% of the total influenced persons.

Considering the viewership, liking and influence on usage it can be concluded that promotional copy is the best, descriptive copy, illustrative copy, USP copy and personality copy stands second, third, fourth and fifth respectively to advertise these four durable consumer goods in newspapers. Competitive copy is a lot lesser effective than personality copy.

Information relating to other durable consumer goods is also collected. It is discussed in Table 3.23.

All the hundred respondents were requested to mention four durable consumer goods other than mobile, motorcycle, washing machine and television whose ad they have seen in newspapers. Thereby 400 names were expected but just 213 names of 34 products were mentioned. Few products' ad are presented here to give better understanding of different ad copies used by them (see Ad 3.74 to 3.94) out of 213 mentioned names 52 are used. Hence we can say the translation of watching ad into sale is 24.41%.

As most of the consumer durables are using a combination of two or more ad copies, it has become necessary to separate these mixed ad copies to find copywise effectiveness of each and every ad copy. Hence Table 3.24 is prepared with the help of Table 3.23.

Considering the data of viewership and influence on usage shown in Table 3.24 it is apparent that promotional copy, descriptive copy and illustrative copy stands first, second and third respectively. USP copy and personality copy are almost equally effective. Straight selling copy stands sixth with unnoticeable contribution.

To find composite effectiveness of each ad copy relating to all consumer durables published in newspaper, Table 3.25 is prepared. Comparative effectiveness of each ad copy is judged by the influence it make on the viewers to buy the product. In this process equal weightage is given to both, the four products (mobile, motorcycle, washing machine and TV) and the other durable products. 7.92%, 5.91%, 4.63%, 2.77%, 2.41%, 0.17% and 0.12% viewers use the advertised durable as they are influenced and stimulated by the promotional copy, descriptive copy, illustrative copy, USP copy, personality copy, straight selling copy and competitive copy respectively. Thus in all 23.93% viewers use the advertised consumer durables.

The overall translation of watching ad into sale shown here in Table 3.25 is very slightly different from the actual figures shown in Table 3.21 and Table 3.23. This is because the overall translation of watching ad into sale here is calculated by the summation of influence of each ad copy and in calculation of separate influence of each ad copy the same person may be counted twice or thrice due to the mixed ad copy used by several products.

Promotional Copy is clearly the most effective ad copy followed by descriptive copy and illustrative copy. Its effectiveness is 34.01% more than descriptive copy and 71.06% more than illustrative copy. USP Copy is 40.17% less effective than illustrative copy but it is 14.94% more influencive than personality copy. Competitive copy and straight selling copy do not make any noticeable effect on Viewers.

ADS WHICH ARE NOT GOOD

All the hundred respondents were requested to mention four products whose ad they do not consider good which are published in newspaper. Thereby 400 names were expected but only 7 respondents could mention 13 names in all. Speed Health Capsule's name was mentioned by four respondents while Body Plus Capsule, Powder Plus Capsule and Nirog Red Tooth Powder's name were mentioned by 3-3 respondents.

When we see these ads in papers we easily find that they are lacking believability. Any rational person will understand that no capsule can develop vigour or build a muscular body like the robust fellow shown in ad. Contribution of any exceptional and extra-ordinary performance of a person cann't be given to a product, this won't do any good to the product.. Readers consider these claims as baseless and fake.

SIZE OF AD

When respondents were asked about the size of ads in newspaper 44% suggested that the ad should be of less than quarter page, 35% said it should be quarter page, 12% said it should be half page and 9% suggested that it should be of full page.

4 Ad Copies in Magazines and Their Effect

Magazine is an important publication media through which several ads are presented. Magazines deliver the advertising message to a measurable group of readers in combination with news, entertainment and other editorial content.

An effort is made to find the effectiveness of different kinds of ad copies relating to different consumer durables and non-durables published in magazines.

TEA

Respondents mentioned three tea brands, that they have seen in magazines. These brands mostly used following kind of ad copy prior to and during the research period. Description of these ads will help in understanding their analysis.

Taj Mahal

It uses personality and illustrative copy in the magazine ads the picture of tea garden is shown and the famous tabla player Ustad Zakir Hussain praises Taj Mahal Tea.

Wagh Bakri

It uses illustrative copy to present its ad. In a ad a young man and lady are shown enjoying Wagh Bakri Tea.

Today

It uses promotional copy in the ads. It is shows in ad that one may win gold chain, gold pendant, washing machine, TV, Camera, Juicer Mixer Grinder, Walkman, Wrist Watch etc. on purchase of Today Premium Tea.

During research all the hundred respondents were requested to fill four blank spaces with the name of tea whose ad they have seen in magazine. Thereby 400 names were expected but respondents mentioned just 22 names.

According to Table 4.1 out of 10 persons who are using the tea of mentioned three brands 4 are such who have not seen any ad in magazine and still using it and in future out of 10 users 5 such persons will be there.

In all 6 persons are using and 5 persons will use the tea whose ad they have seen. As far as these three brands are concerned, magazine ads are contributing 60% to the sale and in future ads will contribute 50% to the sale. Thus the magazine ads are making reasonable contribution in sale but it is declining.

To find the copywise effectiveness of each and every ad copy Table 4.2 is prepared with the help of Table 4.1.

Table 4.2 reveals illustrative, personality and

promotional copy are seen by 19, 12 and 3 persons respectively. In other words they are seen by 55.88%, 35.30% and 8.82% viewers respectively.

Illustrative, personality and promotional copy come first, second and third as 8, 5 and 1 person liked them respectively. It shows illustrative, personality and promotional copy are liked by 57.14%, 35.72% and 7.14% of the total 14 persons who liked the ad.

As far as copywise effect of ad on sale of tea is concerned illustrative, personality and promotional copy stands 1st, 2nd and 3rd by influencing 5, 3 and 1 person respectively i.e. 55.56%, 33.33% and 11.11% of the total 9 influenced persons.

In future illustrative and personality copy stands first and second by influencing 5 and 3 persons respectively i.e. 62.50% and 3.75% of the total 8 influenced persons. Promotional copy will not influence any person to use tea.

After study and analysis of Table 4.1 and 4.2 it can be said that illustrative copy is the best to advertise tea in magazine. It is most seen and liked besides that its influence on usage i.e. sales is highest. Considering the viewership, liking and influence on usage it can be concluded that personality copy stands second. Promotional copy stands third with very negligible influence.

HAIR OIL

Informations relating to hair oil collected from the schedules are presented in Table 4.3. Respondents mentioned six hair oil brands that they have seen in magazine. These brands mostly used following kind of ad copy prior to and during the research period. Description of these ads will help in understanding their analysis.

Table 4.1 : Effectiveness of ad copies relating to tea published in magazines

Sl. No.	Name of Product	Type of ad copy	Persons saw the ad	Persons liked the ad	Persons saw the ad & using the product	Persons saw & liked the ad and using the product	Persons didn't see the ad but using the product	Persons saw the ad & will use the product	Persons saw & liked the ad and will use the product	Persons didn't see the ad but will use the product
1	2	3	4	5	6	7	8	9	10	11
1.	Taj Mahal	Personality and illustrative	12	5	1	2	3	1	2	3
2.	Wagh	Illustrative	7	3	1	1	1	1	1	2
3.	Today	Promotion	3	1	-	1	-	-	-	-
	Total		22	9	2	4	4	2	3	5

Table 4.2 : Effectiveness of separate ad copies relating to tea published in magazines

Sl. No.	Type of ad copy	Persons the saw ad	Persons liked the ad	Persons saw the ad & using the product	Persons saw & liked the ad and using the product	Persons didn't see the ad but using the product	Persons saw the ad & will use the product	Persons saw & liked the ad and will use the product	Persons didn't see the ad but will use the product
1	2	3	4	5	6	7	8	9	10
1.	Personality	Taj 12	5	1	2	3	1	2	3
2.	Illustrative	Taj 12+W7=19	5+3=8	1+1=2	2+1=3	3+1=4	1+1=2	2+1=3	3+2=5
3.	Promotional	Today 3	1	0	1	0	0	0	0
	Total	34	14	3	6	7	3	5	8

Here Taj=Taj Mahal and W=Wagh Bakri

Vatika

It uses personality and USP Copy. Vatika is an unique coconut oil enriched with heena, amla and lemon, that gives extra nourishment to the hair. The TV actress and brilliant anchor Mandira Bedi endorses Vatika Hair Oil.

Keokarpin

Truncated Copy is generally used to remind viewer, the Keokarpin Oil. It do not tell much about the hair oil but just mention the name and picture of product.

Dabur Amla

It uses illustrative and personality Copy. The picture of *amla* and the bottle of Dabur Amla Hair Oil is illustrated along with the big picture of Karishma Kapoor. Another film actress. Rani Mukherjee also endorses Dabur Amla.

Himtaz Oil

The bottle and outer pack of Himtaz Oil are illustrated. Besides that the picture of a lady having long, thick and black hair is prominently shown. The description of hair oil's effect is also given in the ad.

Emami Beauty Secrets by Madhuri

It is made of a unique combination of amla, almond and castor oil that safeguard, moisturize and strengthen the hair from the root. The ad shows this oil is developed by famous, beautiful and lively film heroine Madhuri Dixit.

Himani Navratan

It is shown that Navaratan is a splendid hair oil that releases tension and headache, stops hair fall and resolve the problem of sleeplessness. Film actor Govinda, Amitabh Bachchan and Shahruk Khan are used during the research period to endorse Himani Navratan Oil. Different gift schemes are also advertised in the ad of Navratan Oil.

During research all the hundred respondents were requested to fill four blank spaces with the name of hair oil whose ad they have seen in magazine. Thereby 400 names were expected but respondents mentioned just 58 names.

According to Table 4.3 out of 28 persons who are using the hair oil of mentioned six brands 13 are such who have not seen any ad in magazine and still using it. In future out of 30 users 13 such persons will be there.

In all IS persons are using and 17 persons will use the hair oil whose ad they have seen in magazine. It implies that the ads will contribute in future to increase sale by 13.33%.

As far as these six brânds are concerned, magazine ads are contributing 53.57% to the sale and in future ads will contribute 56.67%. Thus the influence of ad both at present and in future is quite positive.

As most of the hair oil brands are using a combination of two or more ad copies, it has become necessary to separate these mixed ad copies to find the copy wise effectiveness of each and every ad copy. Hence the Table 4.4 is prepared with the help of Table 4.3.

Table 4.4 reveals personality, USP, illustrative and promotional copy are seen by 52, 33, 21 and 12 persons respectively. In other words personality, USP, illustrative and promotional copy are seen by 41.94%, 26.61%, 16.94%, 9.68% viewers respectively. Truncated and descriptive copy are seen by merely 3.22% and 1.61% viewers respectively.

Personality, USP, illustrative and promotional copy are liked by 16, 10, 7 and 3 persons respectively. On the basis of liking personality, USP, illustrative and promotional copy comes 1st, 2nd, 3rd and 4th as they are liked by 43.24%, 27.03%,18.92% and 8.11% of the total 37 persons who liked the ad. Descriptive copy is liked by just 2.70% persons.

As far as copywise effect of ad on sale of hair oil is concerned Personality, USP, illustrative and promotional copy stands 1st, 2nd, 3rd and 4th by influencing 13, 8, 6 and 2 persons respectively to use the advertised hair oil, i.e. 41.93%, 25.81%, 19.35% and 6.45% of the total 31 influenced persons. Truncated and descriptive copy influenced I lone person each to use the advertised hair oil.

In future personality, USP, illustrative, promotional, truncated and descriptive copy influence 14, 9, 6, 2, 2 and 1 person to use the advertised hair oil i.e. 41.18%, 26.47%,17.65%, 5.88%, 5.88% and 2.94% of the total 34 influenced persons.

According to Table 4.4 total number of persons are much more than the actual number of persons because the same persons are counted twice or thrice due to the mixed ad copy used by different hair oil brands.

After study and analysis of Table 4.3 and Table 4.4 it can be said that personality copy is the best to advertise hair oil in magazine. It is most seen and liked besides that its influence on usage i.e. sales is highest. Considering the viewership, liking and influence on

Table 4.3 : Effectiveness of ad copies relating to hair oil published in magazines

Sl. No.	Name of Product	Type of ad copy	Persons saw the ad	Persons liked the ad	Persons saw the ad & using the product	Persons saw & liked the ad and using the product	Persons didn't see the ad but using the product	Persons saw the ad & will use the product	Persons saw & liked the ad and will use the product	Persons didn't see the ad but will use the product
1	2	3	4	5	6	7	8	9	10	11
1.	Vatika	Person-ality & USP	16	5	2	2	4	2	3	5
2.	Keokarpin	Truncated	4	-	1	-	4	2	-	3
3.	Dabur Amla	Person-ality & Illustrative	19	6	2	3	3	2	3	4
4.	Himtaz Oil	Illustra-tive & Descriptive	2	1	-	1	-	-	1	-

5.	Emami Beauty secret by Madhuri	Person-ality & USP	5	2	1	1	-	1	1	-
6.	Himani Navratan	Person-lity, USP & Promotional	12	3	1	1	2	1	1	1
Total			58	17	7	8	13	8	9	13

Table 4.4 : Effectiveness of separate ad copies relating to hair oil published in magazines

Sl. No.	Type of ad copy	Persons the saw ad	Persons liked the ad	Persons saw the ad & using the product	Persons saw & liked the ad and using the product	Persons didn't see the ad but using the product	Persons saw the ad & will use the product	Persons saw & liked the ad and will use the product	Persons didn't see the ad but will use the product
1	2	3	4	5	6	7	8	9	10
1.	Personality	V16+D19+B5 +N12=52	5+6+2+ 3=16	2+2+1 +1=6	2+3+1+ 1=7	4+3+0+ 2=9	2+2+1+ 1=6	3+3+1+ 1=8	5+4+0+ 1=10
2.	USP	V16+B5+N12 =33	5+2+3= 10	2+1+1 =4	2+1+1 =4	4+0+2 =6	2+1+1 =4	3+1+1 =5	5+0+1 =6
3.	Truncated	K4	0	1	0	4	2	0	3
4.	Illustrative	D19+H2=21	6+1=7	2+0=2	3+1=4	3+0=3	2+0=2	3+1=4	4+0=4
5.	Descriptive	H2	1	0	1	0	0	1	0
6.	Promotional	N12	3	1	1	2	1	1	1
	Total	124	37	14	17	24	15	19	24

Here V=Vatika, K=Keokarpin, D=Dabur Amla, H=Himtaz, B= Emami Beauty Secret by Madhuri & N=Himani Navratan usage it can be concluded that USP, illustrative and promotional copy stands second, third and fourth respectively. While truncated and descriptive copy stands fifth and sixth with very little effectiveness.

DETERGENT POWDER

Informations relating to detergent powder's ad collected from the schedules are presented in Table 4.5. Respondents mentioned three detergent powder brands that they have seen in magazines. These brands mostly used following type of ad copy prior to and during the research period. Description of these ads will help in understanding their analysis.

Fena

It uses illustrative and USP copy. The packing of Fena Detergent Powder and Cake and a lady happy with the cleansing of Fena. It highlights the unique triple action enzymes and fabric brightener formula of Fena that will clean and shine the clothes.

Ghari

Just like newspaper ads Ghari uses illustrative and straight selling copy in magazines also. It urges the viewers to use Ghari detergent which is an outcome of ongoing scrupulous research as shown in the picture of a laboratory.

Neo

Without any trick or ploy it straight way present the product in the ad.

During research all the hundred respondents were requested to till four blank spaces with the name of detergent powder whose ad they have seen in magazine. Thereby 400 names were expected but respondents mentioned just 26 names.

According to Table 4.5 out of 16 persons who are using the detergent powder of mentioned three brands 8 are such who have not seen any ad in magazine and still using it. In future out of 17 users 7 such persons will be there.

In all 8 persons are using and 10 persons will use the detergent powder whose ad they have seen in magazine. It implies that the ads will contribute in future to increase sale by 25%.

As far as these three brands are concerned, magazine ads are contributing 50% to the sale and in future ads will contribute 58.82%. Thus the influence of ad both at present and in future is quite positive.

As most of the detergent powders are using a combination of two ad copies, it has become necessary to separate these mixed ad copies to find the copywise effectiveness of each and every ad copy. Hence the Table 4.6 is prepared with the help of Table 4.5

Table 4.6 reveals illustrative, straight selling and USP copy are seen by 24, 17 and 9 persons respectively. In other words they are seen by 48%, 34% and 18% viewers respectively.

On the basis of liking illustrative, straight selling and USP copy comes 1st, 2nd and 3rd respectively as they are liked by 50%, 31.25% and 18.75% of the total 16 persons who liked the ad.

As far as copywise effect of ad on sale of detergent powder is concerned illustrative, straight selling and USP copy stands 1st, 2nd and 3rd by influencing 7, 5 and 3 versons respectively to use the advertised

Table 4.5 : Effectiveness of ad copies relating to detergent powder published in magazines

Sl. No.	Name of Product	Type of ad copy	Persons saw the ad	Persons liked the ad	Persons saw the ad & using the product	Persons saw & liked the ad and using the product	Persons didn't see the ad but using the product	Persons saw the ad & will use the product	Persons saw & liked the ad and will use the product	Persons didn't see the ad but will use the product
1	2	3	4	5	6	7	8	9	10	11
1.	Fena	Illustrative & USP	9	3	1	2	1	2	2	1
2.	Ghari	Illustrative & Straight Selling	15	5	2	2	7	2	3	6
3.	Neo	Straight Selling	2	-	1	-	-	1	-	
	Total		26	8	4	4	8	5	5	7

Table 4.6 : Effectiveness of separate ad copies relating to detergent powder in magazines

Sl. No.	Type of ad copy	Persons the saw ad	Persons liked the ad	Persons saw the ad & using the product	Persons saw & liked the ad and using the product	Persons didn't see the ad but using the product	Persons saw the ad & will use the product	Persons saw & liked the ad and will use the product	Persons didn't see the ad but will use the product
1	2	3	4	5	6	7	8	9	10
1.	Illustrative	F9+G15=24	3+5=8	1+2=3	2+2=4	1+7=8	2+2=4	2+3=5	1+6=7
2.	USP	F9	3	1	2	1	2	2	1
3.	Straight Selling	G15+N2=17	5+0=5	2+1=3	2+0=2	7+0=7	2+1=3	3+0=3	6+0=6
	Total	50	16	7	8	16	9	10	14

Here F= Fena, G= Ghari & N=Neo

detergent powder i.e. 46.67%, 33.33% and 20% of the total 15 influenced persons.

In future illustrative, straight selling and USP copy influence 9, 6 and 4 persons to use the advertised detergent powder i.e. 47.37%, 31.58% and 21.05% of the total 19 influenced persons.

According to Table 4.6 total number of persons are much more than the actual number of persons because the same persons are counted twice due to the mixed ad copy used by different detergent powders. After study and analysis of Table 4.5 and Table 4.6 it can be said that illustrative copy is the best to advertise detergent powder in magazine. It is most seen and liked besides that its influence on usage i.e. sales is highest. Considering the viewersing, liking and influence on usage it can be concluded that straight selling and USP copy stands second and third respectively.

SUITING-SHIRTING

Informations relating to suiting-shirting's ad collected from schedules are presented in Table 4.7 respondents mentioned just one suiting-shirting brand that they have seen in magazines. This brand mostly used following type of ad copy prior to and during the research period. It's description will help in understanding the analysis.

Raymond

It uses illustrative copy. The young man dressed up in Raymond Suiting is illustrated in the ad. The man looks graceful and aristocrat in Raymond.

During research all the hundred respondents were requested to fill four blank spaces with the name of suiting-shirting whose ad they have seen in magazines.

Thereby 400 names were expected but respondents could mention merely 26 names. That too of just one brand i.e. Raymond.

According to Table 4.7 out of 22 persons who are using the suiting shirting of mentioned brand 15 are such who have not seen any ad in magazine and still suing it. In future out of 23 users 15 such persons will be there.

Translation of liking into sale

Out of 44 persons who liked the ad published in magazines 20 persons i.e. 45.45% are using the product. In future 21 persons i.e. 47.73% of the persons who liked the ad, will use the product.

Translation of Sheer Watching (excluding liking) into sale

Out of 88 persons who just saw and not liked the ads, 16 persons i.e. 18.18% are using the advertised product. In future 19 persons i.e. 21.59% of the persons who just saw and not liked the ads, will use the product.

Percentage of users who have not seen the ad

Out of 76 persons who are using these four products 40 are such who have not seen the ad in magazine. It means 52.63% users have not seen the ad. In future out of 80 users of these four products 40 will be such who have not seen the ad. It means 50% future users have not seen the ad in magazine.

Contribution of ads into sale

Out of 76 persons who use the product 36 have seen the ad. It means 47.37% users have seen the ads in other words contribution of ads into sale is 47.37%.

Table 4.7 : Effectiveness of different ad copies relating to suiting-shirting published in magazines

Sl. No.	Name of Product	Type of ad copy	Persons saw the ad	Persons liked the ad	Persons saw the ad & using the product	Persons saw & liked the ad and using the product	Persons didn't see the ad but using the product	Persons saw the ad & will use the product	Persons saw & liked the ad and will use the product	Persons didn't see the ad but will use the product
1	2	3	4	5	6	7	8	9	10	11
1.	Raymond	Illustrative	26	10	3	4	15	4	4	15

Table 4.8 : Composite effectiveness of ads relating to tea, hair oil, detergent powder and suiting-shirting published in magazines

Particulars	Tea	Hair Oil	Deter-gent Powder	Suiting Shirting	Total
Persons saw the ad	22	58	26	26	132
Persons liked the ad	9	17	8	10	44
Persons saw the ad and using the product.	2	7	4	3	16
Persons Saw and liked the ad and using the product.	4	8	4	4	20
Persons didn't see the ad but using the product.	4	13	8	15	40
Persons saw the ad and will use the product.	2	8	5	4	19
Persons saw and liked the ad and will use the product.	3	9	5	4	21
Persons didn't see the ad but will use the product.	5	13	7	15	40

Out of 80 persons who will use the product 40 have seen the ad, in other words contribution of ads into sale will be 50%.

To find the composite effectiveness of every single ad copy published in magazine relating to tea, hair oil, detergent powder and suiting-shirting the Table 4.9 is prepared with the help of Table 4.2, Table 4.4, Table 4.6 and Table 4.7.

Table 4.9 reveals illustrative, personality and USP copy are seen by 90, 64 and 42 persons respectively. In other words they are seen by 38.46%, 27.35% and 17.95% viewers respectively. Viewership of other ad copies are much lesser than these three ad copies. Straight selling, promotional, truncated and descriptive copy are seen by 7.27%, 6.41%, 1.71% and 0.85% viewers respectively.

On the basis of liking illustrative, personality and USP Copy comes 1st, 2nd and 3rd as they are liked by 42.86%, 27.27% and 16.88% of the total 77 persons who liked the ads. Straight selling and promotional copy are liked by just 6.49% and 5.20% of the total 77 persons who liked the ad. Descriptive copy is liked by merely 1.30% of the persons who liked the ad. Truncated copy is not liked by anyone.

As far as copywise effect of ad on sale of these four non-durable products are concerned illustrative, personality, USP, straight selling, promotional, truncated and descriptive copy influence 25, 16, 11, 5, 3, 1 and 1 person respectively to use the advertised product i.e. 40.32%, 25.81%,17.74%, 8.07%, 4.84%, 1.61% and 1.61% of the total 62 influenced persons.

In future illustrative, personality, USP, straight Selling, promotional, truncated and descriptive copy influence 28, 17, 13, 6, 2, 2 and 1 person respectively to use the advertised product i.e. 40.58%, 24.64%, 18.84%, 8.69%, 2.90%, 2.90% and 1.45% of the total 69 influenced persons.

According to Table 4.9 total number of persons are much more than the actual number of persons because the same persons are counted twice or thrice due to the mixed ad copies used by different tea, hair oil, detergent powder and suiting-shirting.

Considering the viewership, liking and influence on usage it can be concluded that illustrative, personality and USP copy stands 1st 2nd and 3rd. After that straight selling and promotional copy are lesser effective so they stand fourth and fifth. Truncated and descriptive copy are very little effective.

Information relating to other non durable goods is also collected. It is presented in Table 4.10.

All the hundred respondents were requested to mention non-durable consumer products other than tea, hair oil, detergent powder and suiting-shirting, whose ad they have seen in magazine. Thereby 400 names were expected but respondents could mention just 72 names. It implies very low viewership. Few products ad are presented here to give better understanding of different ad copies used by them. Out of 72 product names mentioned by respondents 20 are used. Hence, the translation of watching ad into sale is 27.78%.

As most of the non-durable products are using a combination of two or more ad copies during and prior to the research period, it has become necessary to separate these mixed ad copies to find copywise effectiveness of each and every ad copy. Hence, Table 4.11 is prepared with the help of Table 4.10.

Table 4.9 : Effectiveness of separate ad copies relating to tea, hair oil, detergent powder and suiting-shirting published in magazines

Sl. No.	Type of ad copy	Persons the saw ad	Persons liked the ad	Persons saw the ad & using the product	Persons saw & liked the ad and using the product	Persons didn't see the ad but using the product	Persons saw the ad & will use the product	Persons saw & liked the ad and will use the product	Persons didn't see the ad but will use the product
1	2	3	4	5	6	7	8	9	10
1.	Personality	T12+H52=64	5+16=21	1+6=7	2+7=9	3+9=12	1+6=7	2+8=10	3+10=13
2.	Illustrative	T19+H21+ D24+S26=90	8+7+8+ 10=33	2+2+3 +3=10	3+4+4 +4=15	4+3+8+ 15=30	2+2+4+ 4=12	3+4+5+ 4=16	5+4+7+ 165=31
3.	Permotional	T3+H12=15	1+3=4	0+1=1	1+1=2	0+2=2	0+1=1	=0+1=1	0+1=1
4.	USP	H33+D9=42	10+3=13	4+1=5	4+2=6	6+1=7	4+2=6	5+2=7	6+1=7
5	Truncated	H4	0	1	0	4	2	0	3
6.	Descriptive	H2	1	0	1	0	0	1	0
7.	Straight Selling	D17	5	3	2	7	3	3	6
	Total	234	77	27	35	62	31	38	61

Here T=Tea, H=Hair Oil,=Detergent Powder and S=Suiting Shirting

Table 4.10 : Effectiveness of ad copies relating to other consumer non-durables published in magazines

Sl. No.	Name of Product	Type of ad Copy	Number of persons saw the ad	Number of person using product
1.	Anne French	Personality and USP	4	2
2.	Ayur	Illustrative and Descriptive	3	1
3.	Cerelac	Illustrative and Descriptive	3	1
4.	Coca Cola	Personality	6	2
5.	Colgate Brush	Illustrative and USP	2	0
6.	Dabur Gulbari	Promotional	1	0
7.	Dabur Honey	Promotional	3	1
8.	Everyuth	Illustrative, USP and Descriptive	4	1
9.	Fair and Lovely	Illustrative and Descriptive	7	2
10.	Fem	Straight Selling	3	1
11.	Gala Brush	Straight Selling and Illustrative	1	0

12.	Gohnson and Gohnson	Truncated and USP	5	2
13.	Glare kitchenware	USP and Illustrative	1	0
14.	Lakme	Illustrative and Descriptive	6	2
15.	Nivea	Illustrative	2	1
16.	Parle	Illustrative and USP	4	1
17.	Pears	Illustrative and USP	2	0
18.	Rasna	Illustrative	4	2
19.	Safi	Illustrative and USP	3	0
20.	Sugar Free	Illustrative and Descriptive	2	0
21.	Vaseline	Illustrative and USP	4	1
22.	Vasmol	Personality and Descriptive	2	0
Total		72	20	

Table 4.11 reveals illustrative copy is the best. It is most seen and its influence is also high. Considering the viewership and influence on usage shown in Table 4.11 USP and descriptive copy are almost equally good. Personality copy stands third. After that truncated, straight selling and promotional copies make little contributions.

To find composite effectiveness of each ad copy relating to all consumer non-durables published in magazines, Table 4.12 is prepared. Comparative effectiveness of each ad copy is judged by the influence it make on the viewers to buy the product. In this process equal weightage is given to both, the four products (tea, hair oil, detergent powder and suiting-shirting) and the other non-durable products.

9.99%, 5.07%, 4.97%, 2.93%, 1.46%, 1.03% and 0.99% viewers use the advertised non-durable as they are influenced and stimulated by the illustrative copy, USP copy, personality copy, descriptive copy, straight selling copy, promotional copy and truncated copy respectively. Thus in all 26.44% viewers use the advertised consumer non-durables.

The overall translation of watching ad into sale shown here in Table 4.12 is neatly 1% lower than the actual figures shown in Table 4.8 and 4.10. This is because the overall translation of watching ad into sale here is calculated by the summation of influence of each ad copy and in calculation of separate influence of each ad copy the same person may be counted twice or thrice due to the mixed ad copy used by several products.

Illustrative copy is clearly the most effective ad copy followed by USP and personality copy which are nearly half effective than the illustrative copy. Descriptive copy is reasonably effective while straight selling, promotional and truncated copy are very little effective.

Just like non-durable consumer goods facts, information and data relating to the four durable consumer goods namely mobile, motorcycle, washing machine and television are collected through the schedules. Herein after product wise facts, information, data and their analysis is presented.

MOBILE PHONE (HANDSETS)

Information relating the ads of mobile phone collected through the schedules are presented in Table 4.13.

Respondents mentioned three brands of mobile phone that they have seen in magazine. These brands mostly used following kind of ad copy prior to and during the research period. Description of these ads will help in understanding their analysis.

Nokia

It uses a combination of illustrative, promotional and descriptive copy. As it is shown in ad 4.31 and 4.32 a price discount of around one thousand rupees can be availed. Different features of mobile like 16.7 million colours, e-mail facility, 2 megapixal camera and music player are mentioned. The big picture of Nokia 6300 handset is given in the ad.

LG

It also uses a combination of illustrative, promotional and descriptive copy. Stereo Phonic speakers worth Rs. one thousand are free with LG Pulse 2500 and 2600. Description of the handset is given it has ten FM Radio station memory, MP 3 player with 120 MB memory,

Table 4.11 : Effectiveness of separate ad copies relating to other consumer non-durables published in magazines

Sl. No.	Type of ad Copy	Name of product (Number of persons saw the ad/number of persons using the product)	Total number of persons saw the ad	Total number of persons using the product
1.	Illustrative	Ayur (3/1) Cerelac (3/1) Colgate Brush (2/0) Everyuth (4/1) Fair and Lovely (7/2) Gola Brush (1/0) Glare Kitchenware (1/0) Lakme (6/2) Nivea (2/1) Parle (4/1) Pears (2/0) Rasna (4/2) Safi (3/0) Sugar Free (2/0) Vaseline (4/1)	48	12
2.	USP	Anne French (4/2) Colgate Brush (2/0) Everyuth (4/1) Gohnson and Gohnson (5/2) Glare Kitchen Ware (1/0) Parle (4/1) Pears (2/0) Safi (3/0) Vaseline (4/1)	29	7
3.	Descriptive	Ayur (3/1) Cerclac (3/1) Exveryuth (4/1) Fair and Lovely (7/2) Lakme (6/2) Sugar Free (2/0) Vasernol (2/0)	27	7

4.	Straight Selling	Fern (3/1) Gala Brush (1/0)	4	1
5.	Promotional	Dabur Gulbari (1/0) Dabur Honey (3/1)	4	1
6.	Personality	Anne French (4/2) Coca Cola (6/2) Vesemol (2/0)	12	4
7.	Truncated	Gohnson and Gohnson (5/2)	5	2

Table 4.12 : Effectiveness of ad copies relating to all consumer non-durables published in magazines

Sl. No	Type of ad copy	Copywise percentage of viewers who saw the ad of tea, hair oil, detergent powder and suiting-shirting*	Copywise translation of watching ad into sale of tea, hair oil, detergent powder and suiting-shirting (in percentage)	Ad influenced users of tea, hair oil, detergent powder and suiting-shirting-(3x4/100)	Copywise percent-age of viewers who saw the ad of other consumer dourables +	Copywise translation of watching ad into sale of other durables (in percentage)+	Ad influenced users of other durables (6x7/100)	Average ad influence users [(5+8)/2]
1	2	3	4	5	6	7	8	9
1.	Illustrative	38.46	27.78	10.68	37.21	25	9.30	9.99
2.	USP	17.95	26.19	4.70	22.48	24.14	5.43	5.07
3.	Personality	27.35	25	6.84	9.30	33.33	3.10	4.97
4.	Descriptive	0.85	50	0.43	20.93	25.93	5.43	2.93
5.	Straight Selling	7.27	29.41	2.14	3.10	25	0.78	1.46
6.	Promotional	6.41	20	1.28	3.10	25	0.78	1.03
7.	Truncated	1.71	25	0.43	3.88	40	1.55	0.99
	Total	100		26.50	100		26.37	26.44

* Percentage are calculated from the data of Table 4.9.
\+ Percentage are calculated from the data of Table 4.11.

Table 4.13 : Effectiveness of ad copies relating to mobile phone published in magazines

Sl. No.	Name of Product	Type of ad copy	Persons saw the ad	Persons liked the ad	Persons saw the ad & using the product	Persons saw & liked the ad and using the product	Persons didn't see the ad but using the product	Persons saw the ad & will use the product	Persons saw & liked the ad and will use the product	Persons didn't see the ad but will use the product
1	2	3	4	5	6	7	8	9	10	11
1.	Nokia	Illustrative, Promotional & Descriptive	25	9	4	5	26	4	6	29
2.	LG	Illustrative, Promotional & Descriptive	17	6	2	2	6	3	2	6
3.	Samsung	Illustrative and USP	6	3	1	1	11	1	2	11
	Total		48	18	7	8	43	8	10	46

zoom camera, recording and pen drive facility. The picture of mobile and free speakers are illustrated.

Samsung

It generally uses USP and illustrative copy to advertise in magazines e.g. in the ad 4.35 the world's first TFT-LCD colour phone is shown and to highlight this uniqueness a colourful butterfly made from the Samsung mobiles hold by a boy and an elated girl, is illustrated.

During research all the 100 respondents were requested to fill four blank spaces with the name of mobile phone whose ad they have seen in magazine. Thereby 400 names were expected but respondents could mention just 48 names.

According to Table 4.13 out of 58 respondents who are using the mobile of mentioned three brands 43 are such who have not seen any ad in magazine and still using it. In future out of 64 users 46 such persons will be there.

In all 15 persons are using and 18 persons will use the mobile whose ad they have seen in magazine. It implies that the ads will contribute in future to increase sale by 20%.

As far as these three brands are concerned, magazine ads are contributing 25.86% to the sale and in future ads will contribute 28.13% to the sale. Thus the magazine ads are contributing around one-fourth of the total sale of these three brands, which is quite reasonable.

As all the mobile brands are using a combination of two or more ad copies so it has become necessary to separate these mixed ad copies to find the copywise effectiveness of each and every ad copy. Hence, Table 4.14 is prepared with the help of Table 4.13.

Table 4.14 reveals illustrative, promotional and descriptive copy are seen by 48, 42 and 42 persons respectively. In other words they are seen by 34.78%, 30.44% and 30.44% viewers respectively. USP Copy is seen by just 4.34% viewers.

On the basis of liking illustrative copy is the best as it is liked by 35.30% of the total 51 persons who liked the ads. Both the promotional and descriptive copy comes second as they are liked by 29.41%-29.41% of the total 51 persons who liked the ads. While USP copy is liked by just 5.88% persons.

As far as copywise effect of ad on sale of mobile is concerned illustrative, promotional, descriptive and USP copies influence 15, 13, 13 and 2 persons respectively to use the advertised mobile i.e. 34.89%, 30.23%, 30.23% and 4.65% of the total 43 influenced persons.

In future illustrative, promotional, descriptive and USP copies will influence 18, 15, 15 and 3 persons respectively to use the advertised mobile i.e. 35.30%, 29.41%, 29.41% and 5.88% of the total 51 influenced persons.

Here in analysis of Table 4.15 total number of persons are much more than the actual persons because the same persons are counted twice or thrice due to the mixed ad copy used by different mobile phones.

After study and analysis of Table 4.13 and Table 4.14 it can be said that illustrative copy is the best to advertise mobile in magazine. It is used by all the three brands mentioned by viewers. Promotional and descriptive copy jointly stand second. While USP Copy

Table 4.14 : Effectiveness of separate ad copies relating to mobile phone published in magazines

Sl. No.	Type of ad copy	Persons the saw ad	Persons liked the ad	Persons saw the ad & using the product	Persons saw & liked the ad and using the product	Persons didn't see the ad but using the product	Persons saw the ad & will use the product	Persons saw & liked the ad and will use the product	Persons didn't see the ad but will use the product
1	2	3	4	5	6	7	8	9	10
1.	Illustrative	N25+LG17+S6 =48	9+6+3 =18	4+2+1 =7	5+2+1 =8	26+6+ 11=43	4+3+1 =8	6+2+2 =10	29+6+ 11=46
2.	Promotional	N25+LG17 =42	9+6=15	4+2=6	5+2=7	26+6 =32	4+3=7	6+2=8	29+6 =35
3.	Descriptive	N25+LG17=42	9+6=15	4+2=6	5+2=7	26+6 =32	4+3=7	6+2=8	29+6 =35
4.	USP	S6	3	1	1	11	1	2	11
	Total	138	51	20	23	118	23	28	127

Here N=Nokia and S=Samsung

stands third, it is far lesser effective than the previous copies.

MOTORCYCLE

Informations relating to the ads of motorcycle collected from the schedules are presented in Table 4.15. Respondents mentioned two brands of motorcycle that they have seen in magazine. These brands mostly used following kind of ad copy prior to and during the research period. Description of these as will help in understanding their analysis.

Hero Honda

A unique innovative feature of Hero Honda motorcycle is highlighted in the ads e.g. in Hero Honda Super Splendor the unique quantum core engine, in Hero Honda passion and Glamour the stylish graphics and aesthetic looks are highlighted. Besides the description of unique feature other feature are also mentioned. The eye catching picture of motorcycle is always illustrated in the ad.

Super Splendor is presented as 'Sarvgun Sumpann'. Its better power 9 bhp and 125 cc, better mileage and better maintenance (3 years warranty) and quantum core engine are specifically mentioned.

Bajaj

It uses a combination of illustrative, USP and descriptive copy. An impressive picture of Bajaj Motorcycle is illustrated in the ads. It emphasizes unique innovative feature of motorcycle e.g. disc brake, dtsi technology, alloy wheel, cruiser/muscular look etc. A brief description of motorcycle is also given in the ads.

During research all the hundred respondents were requested to fill four blank spaces with the name of motorcycle whose ad they have seen in magazine. Thereby 400 names were expected but respondents could mention just 34 names.

According to Table 4.15 out of 45 respondents who are using the motorcycle of mentioned two brands 34 are such who have not seen any ad in magazine and still using it. In future out of 53 users 37 such persons will be there.

In all 11 persons are using the 16 persons will use the motorcycle whose ad they have seen in magazine. It implies that the ads will contribute in future to increase sale by 45.45%.

As far as these two brands are concerned, magazine ads are attributing 24.44% to the total sale and in future ads will contribute 30.19% to the total sale. Thus the influence of ad both at present and in future is quite reasonable.

One thing is noticeable here that only illustrative, USP and descriptive copy are remembered by the respondents and they are equally effective.

WASHING MACHINE

Informations relating to the ads of washing machine collected from the schedules are presented in Table 4.16. Respondents mentioned three brands of washing machine that they have seen in magazines. These brands mostly used following kinds of ad copy prior to and during the research period. Description of these ads will help in understanding their analysis.

Table 4.15 : Effectiveness of different ad copies relating to motor cycle published in magazines

Sl. No.	Name of Product	Type of ad copy	Persons saw the ad	Persons liked the ad	Persons saw the ad & using the product	Persons saw & liked the ad and using the product	Persons didn't see the ad but using the product	Persons saw the ad & will use the product	Persons saw & liked the ad and will use the product	Persons didn't see the ad but will use the product
1	2	3	4	5	6	7	8	9	10	11
1.	Hero Honda	Illustrative, USP and Descriptive	16	5	3	2	23	4	3	24
2.	Bajaj	Illustrative, USP and Descriptive	18	7	4	2	11	5	4	13
	Total		34	12	7	4	34	9	7	37

Samsung

It uses a combination of illustrative, USP and descriptive copy. A youthful preety young couple is shown happy with Samsung washing machine. A description of its unique and novel Silver Nano technology is given in the ad. Its cleansing gives 99.99% bacteria free clothes and they remain bacteria free for 30 days. In few ads digital and intelligent washing technique is highlighted.

Videocon

A big three dimensional picture of Videocon washing machine is illustrated along with a description of its functioning and features.

LG

It emphasizes an unique revolutionary 'Fabricare System' that gently clean the clothes. A description of its functioning is also given in the ads. A picture of young and naturally beautiful lady is illustrated to suggest that the clothes will remain new and attractive if they are always washed in LG fabricare washing machine just like the young lady shown here.

During research all the hundred respondents were requested to fill four blank spaces with the name of washing machine whose ad they have seen in magazine. Thereby 400 names were expected but respondents could mention just 37 names.

According to Table 4.16 out of 22 respondents who are using the washing machine of mentioned three brands 15 are such who have not seen any ad in magazine and still using it. In future out of 28 users 19 such persons will be there.

In all 7 persons are using and 9 persons will use the washing machine whose ad they have seen in magazine it implies that ads will contribute in future to increase sale by 28.57%.

As far as these three brands are concerned, magazine ads are contributing 31.82% to the sale and in future ads will contribute 32.14% to the sale. Thus the influence of ad both at present and in future is quite reasonable.

As most of the washing machines are using a combination of two or more ad copies, it has become necessary to separate these mixed ad copies to find the copywise effectiveness of each and every ad copy hence the Table 4.17 is prepared with the help of Table 4.16.

Table 4.17 reveals illustrative, descriptive and USP copy are seen by 39.36%, 39.36% and 21.28% viewers respectively.

Illustrative, descriptive and USP copy are liked by 38.46%, 38.46% and 23.08% of the total 26 persons who liked the ads.

As far as copywise effect of ad on sale of washing machine is concerned illustrative, descriptive and USP copy influence 7, 7, 3 persons respectively to use the advertised washing machine i.e. 41.18%, 41.18% and 17.64% of the total 17 influenced persons.

In future illustrative, descriptive and USP copy will influence 9, 9 and 5 persons respectively to use the advertised washing machine i.e. 39.13%, 39.13% and 21.74% of the total 23 influenced persons. According to Table 4.17 total number of persons are much more than the actual number of persons because the same persons are counted twice or thrice due to the mixed ad copy used by different washing machines.

After study and analysis of Table 4.16 and Table 4.17 it can be said that illustrative copy and descriptive copy are the best to advertise washing machine in magazine. After that USP copy comes second.

TELEVISION SET

Informations relating to ads of tv set collected from the schedules are presented in Table 4.18. Respondents mentioned two brands of tv that they have Seen in magazine. These brands mostly used following kind of ad copy prior to and during the research period. Description of these ads will help in understanding their analysis.

LG

Ads of LG TV prominently highlighted the digital golden eye technology that gives no stress to the eyes of viewer. Description of this golden eye technology is also given in the ads to give a sound logical base to the ads. The picture of eyes is illustrated to quickly grab the attention of reader. LG generally uses a combination of USP, illustrative and descriptive copy.

Akai

Different technical features of tv are mentioned in the ad to give better understanding of Akai TV. The big picture of Akai TV and a Sumo Wrestler are illustrated in the ad to highlight the big 29 inches tv, Akai present itself as the only big screen tv.

During research all the hundred respondents were requested to fill four blank spaces with the name of tv sets whose ad they have seen In magazine. Thereby 400 names were expected but respondents could mention just 17 names.

Table 4.16 : Effectiveness of ad copies relating to washing machine published in magazines

Sl. No.	Name of Product	Type of ad copy	Persons saw the ad	Persons liked the ad	Persons saw the ad & using the product	Persons saw & liked the ad and using the product	Persons didn't see the ad but using the product	Persons saw the ad & will use the product	Persons saw & liked the ad and will use the product	Persons didn't see the ad but will use the product
1	2	3	4	5	6	7	8	9	10	11
1.	Samsung	Illustrative, USP and Descriptive	6	2	-	1	3	1	1	3
2.	Videocon	Illustrative, USP and Descriptive	17	4	3	1	7	3	1	11
3.	LG	Illustrative, USP and Descriptive	14	4	1	1	5	2	1	5
	Total		37	10	4	3	15	6	3	19

Table 4.17 : Effectiveness of separate ad copies relating to washing machine published in magazines

Sl. No.	Type of ad copy	Persons the saw ad	Persons liked the ad	Persons saw the ad & using the product	Persons saw & liked the ad and using the product	Persons didn't see the ad but using the product	Persons saw the ad & will use the product	Persons saw & liked the ad and will use the product	Persons didn't see the ad but will use the product
1	2	3	4	5	6	7	8	9	10
1.	Illustrative	All three 37	10	4	3	15	6	3	19
2.	USP	S6+LG14=20	2+4=6	0+1=1	1+1=2	3+5=8	1+2=3	1+1=2	3+5=8
3.	Descriptive	All three 37	10	4	3	15	6	3	19
	Total	94	26	9	8	38	15	8	46

Here S=Samsung

According to Table 4.18 out of 20 respondents who are using the tv of mentioned two brands 16 are such who have not seen any ad in magazine and still using it. In future out of 23 users 18 such persons will be there.

In all four persons are using and five persons will use the tv whose ad they have seen in magazine. It implies that the ads will contribute in future to increase sale by 25%.

As far as these two brands are concerned, magazine ads are contributing 20% to the sale and in future ads will contribute 21.74% to the sale. Thus the magazine ads contribute around one fifth of the sale of these two brands, which is quite reasonable.

One thing is noticeable here that only illustrative, USP and descriptive copy are remembered by the respondents and they are equally effective.

To find composite effectiveness of ads relating to mobile, motorcycle, washing machine and tv published in magazine, Table 4.19 is prepared with the help of Tables 4.13, 4.15, 4.16, 4.18.

Table 4.19 is analysed on the basis of five points mentioned below:

1. **Translation of watching ad into sale**—Out of 136 persons who saw the ads of these four durable products 37 are using these products. That means 27.21% viewers are using the product whose ad they saw. In future 48 persons will use these products out of 136 persons who saw the ad that means 35.29% viewers will use the advertised product.
2. **Translation of liking into sale**—Out of 46 persons who liked itali published in magazine 18 persons i.e. 39.13% are using the product.

In future 24 persons i.e. 52.17% of the persons who liked the ad, will use the product.

3. **Translation of sheer watching (excluding liking) into sale**—Out of 90 persons who just saw and not liked the ad, 19 persons i.e. 21.11% are using the advertised product. In future 24 persons i.e. 26.67% of the persons who just saw and not liked the ad, will use the product.

4. **Percentage of users who have not see the ad**—145 persons are using these four products and out of these 145 persons 108 are such who have not seen the ad in magazine. It means 74.48% users have not seen the ad.

   In future out of 168 users of these four products 120 will be such who have not seen the ad. It means 71. 43% future users have not seen the ad.

5. **Contribution of ads into sale**—Out of 145 persons who use the product 37 have seen the ad. It means 25.52% users have seen the ads, in other words contribution of ads into sale is 25.52%.

Out of 168 persons who will use the product 48 persons have seen the ads. It means 28.57% future users have seen the ad, in other words contribution of ads into sale will be 28.57%.

To find composite effectiveness of every single ad copy, published in magazine relating to mobile, motorcycle, washing machine and tv the Table 4.20 is prepared with the help of Tables 4.14, 4.15, 4.17 and 4.18.

Table 4.20 reveals illustrative, descriptive, USP and promotional copy are 35.32%, 33.77%, 20% and 10.91% of the total 385 viewers.

Table 4.18 : Effectiveness of ad copies relating to television published in magazines

Sl. No.	Name of Product	Type of ad copy	Persons saw the ad	Persons liked the ad	Persons saw the ad & using the product	Persons saw & liked the ad and using the product	Persons didn't see the ad but using the product	Persons saw the ad & will use the product	Persons saw & liked the ad and will use the product	Persons didn't see the ad but will use the product
1	2	3	4	5	6	7	8	9	10	11
1.	LG	Illustrative, USP & Descritive	12	4	1	2	12	1	2	14
2.	Akai	Illustrative, USP & Descriptive	5	2	-	1	4	-	2	4
Total			17	6	1	3	16	1	4	18

Table 4.19 : Composite effectiveness of ad relating to mobile, motorcycle, washing machine and TV published in magazines

Particular	Mobile	Motor Cycle	Washing Machine	Television	Total
Persons saw the ad	48	34	37	17	136
Persons liked the ad	18	12	10	6	46
Persons saw the ad and using the product	7	7	4	1	19
Persons saw and liked the ad and using the product	8	4	3	3	18
Persons didn't see the ad but using the product	43	34	15	16	108
Persons saw the ad and will use the product	8	9	6	1	24
Persons saw and liked ad and will use the product	10	7	3	4	24
Persons didn't see the ad but will use the product	46	37	19	18	120

On the basis of liking illustrative, descriptive, USP and promotional copy comes 1st, 2nd, 3rd and 4th as they are liked by 35.12%, 32.82%, 20.61% and 11.45% of the total 131 persons who liked the ads.

As far as copywise effect of ad on sale of these four durable products are concerned illustrative, descriptive, USP and promotional copy influence 37, 35, 20 and 13 persons respectively to use the advertised product i.e. 35.24%, 33.33%, 19.05% and 12.38% of the total 105 influenced persons.

In future illustrative, descriptive, USP and promotional copy will influence 48, 45, 29 and 15 persons respectively to use these four advertised products i.e. 35.03%, 32.85%, 21.17% and 10.95% of the total 137 influenced persons.

According to Table 4.20 total number of persons are much more than the actual number of persons because the same persons are counted twice or thrice due to the mixed ad copies used by different mobile, motorcycle, washing machine and tv sets.

Considering the viewership, liking and influence on usage it can be concluded that illustrative and descriptive copy stand first and second. After that USP and promotional copy are lesser effective so they stand third and fourth.

Information relating to the ads of other durable consumer goods is also collected it is presented in Table 4.21.

All the hundred respondents were requested to mention durable consumer products other than mobile, motorcycle, washing machine and TV, whose ad they have seen in magazine. Thereby 400 names were expected but respondents could mention just 32 names. It implies very low viewership. Few products ad are

Table 4.20 : Effectiveness of separate ad copies relating to mobile, motor cycle, washing machine and tv published in magazines

Sl. No.	Type of ad copy	Persons the saw ad	Persons liked the ad	Persons saw the ad & using the product	Persons saw & liked the ad and using the product	Persons didn't see the ad but using the product	Persons saw the ad & will use the product	Persons saw & liked the ad and will use the product	Persons didn't see the ad but will use the product
1	2	3	4	5	6	7	8	9	10
1.	Illustrative	M48+Cy34+ W37+TV17=136	18+12+ 10+6 =46	7+7+4 +1=19	8+4+3+ 3=18	43+34+ 15+16 =108	8+9+6+ 1=24	10+7+3 +4=24	46+37+ 19+18= 120
2.	Promotional	M42	15	6	7	32	7	8	35
3.	Descriptive	M42+Cy34+ W37+TV17=130	15+12+ 10+6 =43	6+7+4 +1=18	7+4+3+ 3=17	32+34+ 15+16 =97	7+9+6+ 1=23	8+7+3+ 4=22	35+37+ 19+18= 109
4.	USP	M6+Cy34+ W20+TV17=77	3+12+6 +6=27	1+7+1 +1=10	1+4+2+ 3=10	11+34+ 8+16 =69	1+9+3+ 1=14	2+7+2+ 4=15	11+37+ 8+18 =74
	Total	385	131	53	52	306	68	69	338

Here M=Mobile, Cy=Motorcycle and W=Washing Machine

presented here to give better understanding of different ad copies used by them. Out of 32 product names mentioned by respondents 9 are used. Hence the translation of watching ad into sale is 28.13%.

As most of the durable products are using a combination of two or more ad copies during and prior to the research period, it has become necessary to separate these mixed ad copies to find copywise effectiveness of each and every ad copy. Hence, Table 4.22 is prepared with the help of Table 4.21.

Considering the data of viewership and influence on usage shown in Table 4.22 it is apparent that illustrative, descriptive and USP copy stands first, second and third respectively. One more thing is also clear that illustrative copy is far more effective than descriptive and USP caples.

To find composite effectiveness of each ad copy relating to all consumer durables published in magazines. Table 4.23 is prepared. Comparative effectiveness of each ad copy is judged by the influence it make on the viewers to buy the product. In this process equal weightage is given to both the four products (mobile phone, motorcycle, washing machine and tv) and the other durable products.

11.73%, 8.39%, 4.91% and 1.69% viewers use the advertised durables as they are influenced and stimulated by the illustrative copy, descriptive copy, USP copy and promotional copy respectively. Thus in all 26.72% viewers use the advertised consumer durables. The overall translation of watching ad into sale shown here in Table 4.23 is a bit different from the actual figures shown in Table 4.19 and 4.22. This is because the overall translation of watching ad into sale here is calculated by the summation of influence of each ad copy and in calculation of separate influence

Table 4.21 : Effectiveness of ad copies relating to other consumer durables published in magazines

Sl. No.	Name of Product	Type of ad copy	Number of persons saw the ad	Number of persons using the product
1.	Hindware	Illustrative	1	0
2.	Johnson Tiles	Illustrative and USP	1	0
3.	Inasla	Illustrative and Descriptive	2	0
4.	Kurlon Mattress	USP	3	0
5.	United Cooker	Illustrative	4	1
6.	Glen Gas Stove	USP and Illustrative	2	0
7.	VIP Suitcase	USP and Illustrative	5	2
8.	HMT	Illustrative	2	1
9.	Videocon Refrigerator	Illustrative and Descriptive	3	1
10.	Springwel Mattress	Illustrative and Descriptive	3	1
11.	Prestige Cooker	Illustrative and Descriptive	6	2
12.	Usha Sewing Machine	Illustrative and Descriptive	4	1
	Total		32	9

Table 4.22 : Effectiveness of separate ad copies relating to other consumer durables published in magazines

Sl. No.	Type of ad copy	Name of product (number of persons saw the ad/number of persons using product)	Total number of persons saw the ad	Total number of persons using product
1.	Illustrative	Hind ware (1/0) Johnson Tiles (1/0) Inalsa (2/0) United Cooker (4/1) Glen Gas Stove (2/0) VIP Suitcase (5/2) HMT (2/1) Videocon Refrigerator (3/1) Springwel Mattress (3/1) Prestige Cooker (6/2) Usha Sewing Machine (4/1)	33	9
2.	Descriptive	Inalsa (2/0) Videocon Refrigerator (3/1) Springwel Mattress (3/1) Prestige Cooker (6/2) Usha Sewing Machine (4/1)	18	5
3.	USP	Johnson tiles (1/0) Kurlon Mattress (3/0) Glen Gas Stove (2/0) VIP Suitcase (5/2) Videocon Refrigerator (3/1).	14	3

Table 4.23 : Effectiveness of different ad copies relating to all consumer durables published in magazines

Sl. No.	Type of Ad	Copywise %age of viewers who saw the ad of mobile, M.cycle, washing machine & TV*	Copywise translation of watching ad into sale of mobile, M.cycle, washing machine & TV* (in %age)	Ad influenced users of mobile, M.cycle, washing machine & TV (3×4/100)	Copywise %age of viewers who saw the ad of other consumer dourable+	Copywise translation of watching ad into sale of other consumer dourable (in %age)+	Ad influenced users of other dourable (6×7/100)	Average ad influence users [(5+8)/2]
1	2	3	4	5	6	7	8	9
1.	Illustrative	35.32	27.21	9.61	50.77	27.27	13.84	11.73
2.	Descriptive	33.77	26.92	9.09	27.69	27.78	7.69	8.39
3.	USP	20	25.97	5.19	21.54	21.43	4.62	4.91
4.	Promotional	10.91	30.95	3.38	-	-	-	1.69
	Total	100		27.27	100		26.15	26.72

* Percentage are calculated from the data of Table 4.20.

\+ Percentages are calculated from the data of Table 4.22.

of each ad copy the same person may be counted twice or thrice due to the mixed ad copy used by several products.

Illustrative copy is clearing the most effective ad copy its effectiveness is 39.81% more than descriptive copy and 138.90% more than USP copy.

ADS WHICH ARE NOT GOOD

One surprising thing that come out of research is that no one really dislike the ads published in magazines as not a single respondent mentioned the name of product whose ad they consider not good.

SIZE OF AD

When respondent were asked about the size of ads in magazine 31% suggested the ad should be of full page, 27% said it should be half page, 24% said it should be quarters page and 18% suggested that it should be of less than quarter page. Hence it is clear that big size ads aresa prefered over small size ads in magazines.

5 Ad Copies on Television and Their Effect

Television is widely seen throughout the country. On an average an urban inhabitant spend about two hours daily in watching TV. Now-a-days different tv channels are running, they cater to the needs of different persons having different tastes and likings. New channels, Entertainment channels, Music channels, Sports channel, Educational channel, Religious channel etc. are broadcasted so the viewership of tv is considerably increased.

Almost in every TV programme few ads are broadcasted in every 10-15 minutes, so the companies can get sound viewership by advertising their product on TV.

In this research facts, information and data relating to the consumer durables and non-durables are collected. Herein after productwise facts, information, data and their analysis is being presented and written.

TEA

Data relating to tea collected from the schedule are presented in Table 5.1.

Respondents mentioned eight tea brands, that they have seen on television. These brands mostly used following kind of ad copy prior to and during the research period. Description of these ads will help understanding their analysis.

Taj Mahal

The famous *'tabla'* player Ustad Zakir Hussain the distinct taste and fragrance of Taj Mahal Tea. Zakir recognizes Taj Mahal Tea amongst several other tea and having a sip of Taj a tremendous glow comes on his face and joyfully says one in thousand tea have such a superb taste. It Taj is a super ordinary and elegant tea.

Tata Tea

It uses drama, USP and personality copy. When friends met, mother of one friend ask them for tea. All says yes one among them don't drink tea so he refused. Once the mother start preparing Tata Tea Gold 'a long leaf tea' its pleasant fragrance read all over the house and the non tea drinker friend start smelling it surprisingly. Then all the friends say "It you refuse, you will have to regret" (ना कहोगे तो पछताओगे)

In the ad of Tata Tea Premium it is showed that Sania Mirza outplayed her opponent with powerful strokes after drinking the tea.

Brooke Bond

It uses poetic, drama and USP copy. A household lady keep herself fresh throughout the day while working, just by drinking Brooke Bond Taza Tea and in that presentation a melodious background song is played "fresh at morning, fresh at evening, fresh at every work throughout the day".

Brooke Bond A One is 'very strong tea'. After having this strong tea a normal and slim lady become emotionally so strong that she sit bravely in fort of a buldozer and stop it moving ahead to demolish a coloney of innocent persons.

Red Label

Through a dramatic persecution it is stated that Red Label tea 'contents *Ashwagandha, Mulethi* and other such *ayurvedic* herbs' that have rich medicinal value.

502-Pataka

In dramatic ad of 502-Pataka Aditi Govitrikar a beautiful actress and model come down from the train and goes to the stall where 502-Pataka tea is available. "The poor persons and train staff who were drinking 502-Pataka wonders that such a big celebrity is also a 502-Pataka fan. From the poor to the rich all find its taste marvelous.

Tez

After drinking Tez tea mother solve difficult problems of mathematics, science and history at extremely rapid pace. Tez do not just give the energy but it unbelievably increases the memory and intelligence of mother. It is sheer exaggeration, no tea can do such wonders.

Today

It uses promotional ad copy. It claims bumper prizes like car, mobile phone etc. will be given to the buyers of Today tea.

Tatley

It also uses promotional ad copy. It says one will certainly get free gifts like tea mugs, audio cassette, bowls etc. on purchase of tatley tea.

During research all the hundred respondents were requested to fill four blank spaces with the name of tea whose ad they have seen on tv. Thereby 400 names were expected but respondents mention just 208 names.

According to Table 5.1 out of 53 persons who are using the tea of mentioned eight brands just 4 are such who have not seen any ad on tv and still using it and in future out of 53 users just 3 such persons will be there.

In all 49 persons are using and 50 persons will use the tea whose ad they have seen. It implies that the ads will contribute in future to increase sale by 2.04%. As far as these eight brands are concerned, tv ads are contributing 92.4,5% to the sale and in future ads will contribute 94.34%. Thus the effect of ad both at present and in future is extremely positive; they are contributing a lot in the sale.

As most of the tea brands are using a combination of two or more ad copies, it has become essential to separate these mixed ad copies to find the copywise effectiveness of each and every ad copy. Hence the Table 5.2 is prepared with the data of Table 5.1.

Table 5.2 reveals 145 blanks are filled with the name of that used drama copy to present its ad. After that 132 and 121 persons have seen the ad of tea that used USP and personality copy respectively. Elegance and poetic copy is seen by 52 and 41 persons while exaggeration and promotional copy are seen by merely 8 and 5 persons respectively. In other words drama,

Table 5.1 : Effectiveness of ad copies relating to tea broadcasted on tv

Sl. No.	Name of Product	Type of ad copy	Persons saw the ad	Persons liked the ad	Persons saw the ad & using the product	Persons saw & liked the ad and using the product	Persons didn't see the ad but using the product	Persons saw the ad & will use the product	Persons saw & liked the ad and will use the product	Persons didn't see the ad but will use the product
1	2	3	4	5	6	7	8	9	10	11
1.	Taj Mahal	Person-ality & Elegance	52	8	4	2	-	4	2	
2.	Tata Tea	Person-ality, Drama & USP	58	24	9	12	1	10	12	1
3.	Brooke Bond	Poetic, Drama & USP	41	14	6	4	-	6	5	-
4.	Red Label	Drama & USP	33	10	5	3	-	5	3	-

5.	502 Pataka	Personality & Drama	11	4	1	1	1	1	1	-
6.	Tez	Exaggeration	8	2	-	1	2	-	1	2
7.	Today	Promotional	3	-	1	-	-	-	-	-
8.	Tatley	Drama & Promotional	2	-	-	-	-	-	-	-
	Total		208	62	26	23	4	26	24	3

USP, personality, elegance and poetic copy are seen by 28.77%, 26.19%, 24.01%, 10,32% and 10.32% viewers respectively. Exaggeration and promotional Copy are seen by merely 1.59% and 0.99% viewers.

Drama, USP and personality copy come first, second and third 52, 48 and 36 persons liked them respectively. Poetic and glance copy are liked by just 14 and 8 persons respectively. Merely 2 persons liked the exaggeration copy while no one liked motional copy. It shows drama, USP, personality, poetic, elegance and exaggeration copy are liked by 32.5%, 30%, 22.5%, 8.75%, 5% and 1.25% of the total 160 persons who liked the ad.

As far as copywise effect of ad on sale of tea is concerned drama, USP, personality, poetic and elegance copy stands first, second, third, fourth and fifth by influencing 41, 39, 29, 10 and 6 persons respectively, i.e. 32.28%, 30.71 %, 22.84%, 7.87% and 4.72% of the total 127 influenced persons. Exaggeration and promotional copy influenced just one person each to use the advertised tea.

In future drama, USP, personality, poetic and elegance copy also stands first, second, third, fourth and fifth by influencing 43, 41, 30, 11 and 6 persons respectively, to use the advertised tea. Influence of exaggeration and promotional copy will be negligible. Influence of ad copies will marginally increase with an exemption of elegance, exaggeration and promotional copy.

Here in analysis of Table 5.2 total number of persons are much more than the actual number of persons because the same person are counted twice or thrice due to the mixed ad copy used by different tea brands.

After study and analysis of Table 5.1 and Table 5.2 it can be said that drama copy is the best to advertise tea on tv. It is most seen and liked besides that its influence on usage i.e sales is highest. Considering the viewership, liking and influence on usage it can be concluded that USP, personality, poetic, elegance, exaggeration and promotional copy stands second, third, fourth, fifth, sixth and seventh respectively.

HAIR OIL

Informations relating to hair oil collected from the schedules are presented in Table 5.3. Respondents mentioned eight hair oil brands that they have seen on tv. These brands mostly used following kind of ad copy prior to and during the research period. Description of these ads will help in understanding their analysis.

Bajaj Almond Drop

It uses poetic and USP copy. The song *'Bajaj Almond Drop Se Balo Ka Kuch Kuch Kare'* is sung and a beautiful model come with different hair styles. Bajaj's Almond Oil enriched with vitamin E gives extra strength to the hair this is emphasised in the ad.

Dabur Vatika

TV actress and anchor Mandira Bedi thanks Vatika for giving *Problem free hair.* Its application nullify the harsh effect of pollution, stop hair falling and their implications.

Dabur Amla

In a poetic background earlier Karishma Kapoor and nowadays Rani Mukherjee praises Dabur Amla. Hair will remain black and become dense and strong by applying Dabur Amla.

Himani Navratan

Through a rhythemic song unique qualities of Himani Navratan Oil ore mentioned. Earlier Govinda, Amitabh Bachchan and nowadays Shahrukh Khan claims it is *so cool that it releases tension, headache and sleeplessness.*

Keokarpin

The ad claims this is a *non sticky hair oil enriched with vitamin E.*

Parachute

Through a dramatic presentation it is showed that parachute is the *purest oil extracted from best coconuts.* Massage with parachute oil give extra long and shiny hair.

Hair & Care

Everyone tease a girl saying '*chipku-chipku*' but after applying hair & care *non sticky hair oil* her total *personality enhances.* From a simpleton looking girl. She becomes smart and gorgeous.

Shanti Amla

It is presented through a melodious song III which the name Shanti Amla is repeated many a times.

During research all the hundred respondents were requested to fill four blank spaces with the name of hair oil whose ad they have seen on tv. Thereby 400 names were expected but respondents mention just 192 names.

According to Table 5.3 out of 58 persons who are using the hair oil of mentioned eight brands just 9 are such who have not seen any ad on tv and still using it. In future out of 65 users just 9 such persons will be there.

In all 49 persons are using and 56 will use the hair oil whose ad they have seen on tv. It implies that the ads will contribute in future to increase sale by 14.29%.

As far as these eight brands are concerned, tv ads are contributing 84.48% to the sale and in future ads will contribute 86.15%. Thus the influence of ad both at present and III future IS extremely positive.

As most of the hair oil brands are using a combination of two or more ad copies, it has become necessary to separate these mixed ad copies to find the copywise effectiveness of each and every ad copy. hence the Table 5.4 is prepared with the help of Table 5.3.

Table 5.4 reveals 155 blanks are filled with the name of hair oil that used USP copy to present its. ad. After that 89, 85 and 62 persons saw the personality, poetic and drama copy respectively. In other words USP, personality, poetic and drama copy is seen by 39.64%, 22.76%, 21.74% and 15.86% viewers respectively.

USP, personality, poetic and drama copy are liked by 49, 30, 27 and 19 persons respectively. On the basis of liking USP, personality, poetic and drama copy comes first, second, third and fourth as they are liked by 39.20, 24%, 21.60% and 15.20% of the total 125 persons who liked the ad.

As far as copywise effect of ad on sale of hair oil is concerned USP, drama, personality and poetic copy stands first, second, third and fourth by influencing 40, 20, 19 and 18 persons respectively to use the advertised hair oil, i.e. 41.24%, 20.62%, 19.59%, and

Table 5.2 : Effectiveness of separate ad copies relating to tea broadcasted on tv

Sl. No.	Type of ad copy	Persons the saw ad	Persons liked the ad	Persons saw the ad & using the product	Persons saw & liked the ad and using the product	Persons didn't see the ad but using the product	Persons saw the ad & will use the product	Persons saw & liked the ad and will use the product	Persons didn't see the ad but will use the product
1	2	3	4	5	6	7	8	9	10
1.	Drama	Tata 58+B1+ R33+P11+ Tatley2=145	24+14+ 10+4+0 =52	9+6+5 +1+0 =21	12+4+3 +0=20	1+0+0+ 1+0 =2	10+6+5 +1+0 =22	12+5+3 1+0 =21	1+0+0+ 0+0 =1
2.	USP	Tata 58+ B41+R33=132	24+14+ 10=48	9+6+5 =20	12+4+3 =19	1+0+0 =1	10+6+5 =21	12+5+3 =20	1+0+0 =1
3.	Personality	Taj 52+Tata 58+P11=121	8+24+4 =36	4+9+1 =14	2+12+1 =15	0+1+1 =2	4+10+1 =15	2+12+1 =15	0+1+0 =1
4.	Poetic	B41	14	6	4	0	6	5	0
5.	Exaggeration	Tez 8	2	0	1	2	0	1	2

6.	Elegance	Taj 52	8	4	2	0	4	2	0
7.	Promotional	Today3+ Tatley2=5	0+0=0	1+0=1	0+0=0	0+0=0	0+0=0	0+0=0	0+0=0
	Total	504	160	66	61	7	68	64	5

Here Taj=Taj Mahal, Tata=Tata Tea, B=Brooke Bond, R=Red Label & P=502 Pataka

18.55% of the total 97 influenced persons.

In future USP, drama, personality and poetic copy stands 1st, 2nd and by influencing 45, 24, 20 and 20 persons respectively i.e. 41.28%, 22.02%,18.35% and 18.35% of the total 109 influenced persons.

According to Table 5.4 the total number of persons are much more than the actual number of persons because the same person is counted twice or thrice due to the mixed ad copy used by different hair oil brands.

After study and analysis of Table 5.3 and Table 5.4 it can be said that USP copy is the best to advertise hair oil on tv. It is most seen and liked besides that its influence on usage i.e. sales is highest. Considering the viewership and liking personality and poetic copy are better than drama copy but on the basis of influence on usage drama copy is ahead of personality and poetic copy.

DETERGENT POWDER

Informations relating to detergent powder's ad collected from the schedules are presented in Table 5.5. Respondents mentioned seven detergent powder brands that they have seen on tv. These brands mostly used following kind of ad copy prior to and during the research period. Description of these ads will help in understanding their analysis.

Nirma

Nirma brings more whiteness in lesser price, that's why it enters in many-many house holds this message IS sung beautifully. Nowadays another song "Hema, Jaya, Rekha and Sushma everyone like Nirma ...." is sung after a drama in which four ladies named Hema, Jaya, Rekha and Sushma play pranks on each oilier.

Surf

By washing clothes with Surf Excel one can *save two bucketful of water* every day as it has a unique *less foaming formula* so little water is required in rinsing clothes. In doing something good children get their clothes dirty with mud, ink or colour, with Surf Excel there is no tension in cleansing all these dirty clothes even one will say 'stains are good, as they are received while doing something good'. Surf remove stain without being harsh on colours of clothes, this is also highlighted in ads.

Ariel

It always uses USP copy. The USP is changed time to time to keep the Ariel always novel and better in the eyes of prospects. It is prominently stated that Ariel not just clean the clothes but it hygienically clean them. Ariel is available in fragrance of two flowers. It has oxy plus formula so it oxygenate the old dry stains and remove them easily.

Tide

Small drama is presented to advertise Tide. In the drama some one is shown happy with his clean white dress but all of a sudden a more white shining strip appear on his shirt and he surprise what make it shine that much., Then a sound comes from the background 'Tide'. Buy Tide and get dazzling whiteness even in just Rupee one. Tide is available in a small sachet of 1 Rs. Reduced price of Tide is also highlighted in the ad.

Wheel

Different dramas are played to advertise wheel. In one such drama a wife asked her husband to buy wheel

Table 5.3 Effectiveness of ad copies relating to hair oil broadcasted on tv

Sl. No.	Name of Product	Type of ad copy	Persons saw the ad	Persons liked the ad	Persons saw the ad & using the product	Persons saw & liked the ad and using the product	Persons didn't see the ad but using the product	Persons saw the ad & will use the product	Persons saw & liked the ad and will use the product	Persons didn't see the ad but will use the product
1	2	3	4	5	6	7	8	9	10	11
1.	Bajaj Almond Drop	Poetic & USP	26	8	2	3	-	3	3	
2.	Vatika	Person-ality & USP	37	13	4	4	-	4	5	1
3.	Dabur Amla	Poetic & Personlity	30	9	5	2	1	5	3	1
4.	Himani Navratan	Poetic, Person-lity & USP	22	8	-	4	-	1	2	

5.	Keokarpin	USP	8	1	2	1	2	2	1	2
6.	Parachute	Drama & USP	53	16	11	6	5	13	7	4
7.	Hair & Care	USP & Drama	9	3	2	1	-	2	2	
8.	Shanti Amla	Poetic	7	2	1	1	1	2	1	1
Total			192	60	27	22	9	32	24	9

Table 5.4 : Effectiveness of separate ad copies relating to hair oil broadcasted on tv

Sl. No.	Type of ad copy	Persons the saw ad	Persons liked the ad	Persons saw the ad & using the product	Persons saw & liked the ad and using the product	Persons didn't see the ad but using the product	Persons saw the ad & will use the product	Persons saw & liked the ad and will use the product	Persons didn't see the ad but will use the product
1	2	3	4	5	6	7	8	9	10
1.	USP	B26+V37+N22 + K8+P53+H9 =155	8+13+8 +1+16+ 3=49	2+4+0 +2+11 +2=21	3+4+4+ 1+6+1= 19	0+0+0+ 2+5+0 =7	3+4+1+ 2+13+2 =25	3+5+2+ 1+7+2 =20	0+1+0+ 2+4+0 =7
2.	Personality	V37+D30+N22 = 89	13+9+8 =30	4+5+0 =9	4+2+4 =10	0+1+0 =1	4+5+1 =10	5+3+2 =10	1+1+0 =2
3.	Poetic	B26+D30+N22 +S7=85	8+9+8+ 2=27	2+5+0 +1=8	3+2+4+ 1=10	0+1+0+ 1=2	13+5+1+ 2=11	13+3+2+ 1=9	0+1+0+ 1=2
4.	Drama	P53+H9=62	16+3 =19	11+2 =13	6+1=7	5+0=5	13+2 =15	7+2=9	4+0=4
	Total	391	125	51	46	15	61	48	15

Here B=Bajaj Alomond Drop, V=Dabur Vatika, D=Dabur Amla, N=Himani Navratan, K=Keokarpin, P=Parachute, H=Hair & Care and S=Shanti Amla but husband denys saying that buy some cheap detergent powder. Then wife says it is not a costly powder and she buys it. Later she cleaned her husband's clothes with wheel. When husband wear them he feel gland and joyfully says you made me an engineer from a mechanic.

Ghari

The song 'first use, then believe...' is sung in the ads of Ghari detergent powder. It is showed that this powder is an outcome of many years research.

Rin Advance

Amitabh Bacchan a famous film actor asked a child that how he get such a dazzling white clothes. The boy innocently reply from Rin Advance.

During research all the hundred respondents were requested to fill four blanks spaces with the name of detergent powder whose ad they have seen on tv. Thereby 400 names were expected but respondents mention just 273 names.

According to Table 5.5 out of 98 persons who are using the detergent powder of mentioned seven brands just 11 are such who have not seen any ad on tv and still using it. In future out of 98 users just 10 such persons will be there.

In all 87 persons are using and 88 persons will use the detergent powder whose ad they have seen on tv.

As far as these seven brands are concerned, tv ads are contributing 88.78% to the sale and in future ads will contribute 89.80%. Thus the influence of ad both at present and in future is extremely positive.

As most of the detergent powders are using a combination of two or more ad copies, it has become necessary to separate these mixed ad copies to find the copywise effectiveness of each and every ad copy. Hence the Table 5.6 is prepared with the help of Table 5.5.

Table 5.6 reveals Drama, poetic, USP, child innocent, promotional and personality copy are seen by 178, 100, 95, 63, 32 and 12 persons respectively. In other words they are seen by 37.08%, 20.83%, 19.79%, 13.13%, 6.67% and 2.50% viewers respectively.

Drama, poetic, USP and child innocent copy are liked by 68, 46, 27 and 21 persons respectively. Promotional and Personality Copy are liked by just 9 and 2 persons.

Oil the basis of liking drama, poetic, USP and child innocent copy comes 1st, 2nd, 3rd and 4th as they are liked by 39.31%, 26.59%, 15.61% and 12.14% of the total 173 persons who liked the ad. Promotional and personality copy are liked by merely 5.20% and 1.15% of the total persons who liked the ad.

As far as copywise effect of ad on sale of detergent powder is concerned drama, poetic, USP, child innocent, promotional and personality copy stands 1st, 2nd, 3rd, 4th, 5th and 6th by influencing 63, 38, 31, 18, 11 and person respectively to use the advertised detergent powder i.e. 38.89%, 23.45%, 19.14%, 11.11%, 6.79% and 0,62% of the total 162 influenced persons. Almost same influence is likely to be seen in future.

According to Table 5.6 total number of persons are much more than the actual number of persons because the same persons are counted twice or thrice due to the mixed ad copy used by different detergents.

After study and analysis of Table 5.5 and 5.6 it can be said that drama copy is the best to advertise detergent powder on tv. It is most seen and liked besides that its influence on usage i.e. sales is highest. Considering the viewership, liking and influence on usage it can be concluded that poetic, USP, child innocent, promotional and personality copy stand 2nd, 3rd, 4th, 5th and 6th respectively. Promotional and personality copy are far lesser effective than the first four ad copies.

SUITING SHIRTING

Informations relating to suiting- shirting's ad collected from the schedules are presented in Table 5.7. Respondents mentioned six brands of suiting-shirting that they have seen on tv. These brands mostly used following kind of ad copy prior to and during the research period. Description of these ads will help in understanding their analysis.

Raymond

A man look superb and graceful in Raymond Suiting-Shirting. His personality enhances and he grab the attention of everyone. The ad shows that Raymond is really a high class and aristocrat fabric. The man look complete and perfect in Raymond dressing.

Siyaram

The song come home to Siyaram is played in the ad. Siyaram's Fabric named Mistair is a *Fabric that breathes.* This unique quality of Mistrair keep the body cool. Even in hot summers one can joyfully wear the suit.

Grasim

Husband and wife quarrel on something. The wife crush the coat and pant of her husband in anger and

Table 5.5 : Effectiveness of ad copies relating to detergent powder broadcasted on tv

Sl. No.	Name of Product	Type of ad copy	Persons saw the ad	Persons liked the ad	Persons saw the ad & using the product	Persons saw & liked the ad and using the product	Persons didn't see the ad but using the product	Persons saw the ad & will use the product	Persons saw & liked the ad and will use the product	Persons didn't see the ad but will use the product
1	2	3	4	5	6	7	8	9	10	11
1.	Nirma	Poetic & Drama	72	34	16	13	5	16	14	5
2.	Surf'	Child Innocent, Drama & USP	51	19	10	7	1	10	7	1
3.	Ariel	USP	44	8	10	4	1	11	4	1 4
4.	Tide	Drama & Promo tional	32	9	7	4	0	6	3	0

5.	Wheel	Drama	23	6	5	1	2	5	1	1
6.	Ghari	Poetic	28	12	5	4	2	5	4	2
7.	Rin Advance	Person-ality & Child Innocent	12	2	0	1	0	1	1	0
	Total		262	90	53	34	11	54	34	10

Table 5.6 : Effectiveness of separate ad copies relating to detergent powder broadcasted on tv

Sl. No.	Type of ad copy	Persons the saw ad	Persons liked the ad	Persons saw the ad & using the product	Persons saw & liked the ad and using the product	Persons didn't see the ad but using the product	Persons saw the ad & will use the product	Persons saw & liked the ad and will use the product	Persons didn't see the ad but will use the product
1	2	3	4	5	6	7	8	9	10
1.	Drama	N72+S51+T32+ W23=178	34+19+ 9+6=68	16+10+ 7+5=38	13+7+4 +1=25	5+1+0+ 2=8	16+10+ 6+5=37	114+7+3 +1=25	55+1+0+ 1=57
2.	USP	S51+A44=95	19+8 =27	10+10 =20	7+4=11	1+1=2	10+11 =21	7+4=11	1+1=2
3.	Poetic	N72+G28=100	34+12 =46	16+5 =21	13+4 =17	5+2=7	16+5 =21	14+4 =18	5+2=7
4.	Child Innocent	S51+R12=63	19+2 =21	10+0 =10	7+1=8	1+0=1	10+1 =11	7+1=8	1+0=1
5.	Promotional	T32	9	7	4	0	6	3	0
6.	Personality	R12	2	0	1	0	1	1	10
Total		480	173	96	66	18	97	66	17

Here N=Nirma, S=Surf, A=Ariel, T=Tide, W=Wheel, G=Ghari & Rin Advance.

throw them on the bed. Husband take them and put on gracefully. No wrinkle comes on the suit and looking that both husband and wife start smiling. The unique *uncrushable* quality of Grasim is presented through this drama.

Mayur

the jingle *'Kya hit Kya Fit.....Mayur'* is played and film actor Shahrukh Khan comes in different suits and proudly tell his name Shahrukh Mayur Khan giving all credit of his charming personality to Mayur Suiting. Nowadays blazing cricketer Virendra Sehwag endorses Mayur in place of Shahrukh Khan.

Reid & Taylor

Just by wearing Reid & Taylor Suitings the sixty year old Amitabh Bachhan perform impossible stunts, even the bullets and fire cann't do any harm to him. He is presented as a super hero and he gets that super power and energy from Reid & Taylor.

BSL

Through a dramatic presentation it is showed that a beautiful and charming film actress Sonali Bendrea attracts towards a person dressed up in BSL Suiting.

During research all the hundred respondents were requested to fill four blank spaces with the name of suiting-shirting whose ad they have seen on tv. Thereby 400 names were expected but respondents could mention just 234 names.

According to Table 5.7 out of 73 persons who are using the suiting-shirting of mentioned six brands just 19 are such who have not seen and ad on tv and still using it. In future out of 78 users just 12 such persons will be there.

In all 54 persons are using and 66 persons will use the suiting shirting whose ad they have seen on tv. It implies that the ads will contribute in future to increase sale by 22.22%.

As far as these six brands are concerned, tv ads are contributing 73.97% to the sale and in future ads will contribute 84.62%. Thus influence of ad both at present and in future is highly positive.

As most of the suiting-shirting brands are using a combination of two or more ad copies, it has become necessary to separate these mixed ad copies to find the copywise effectiveness of each and every ad copy. Hence the Table 5.8 is prepared with the help of Table 5.7.

Table 5.8 reveals poetic, USP, personality, elegance, drama and exaggeration copy are seen by 93, 89, 77, 68, 59 and 14 persons respectively. In other words they are seen by 23.25%, 22.25%, 19.25%, 17%, 14.75% and 3.50% viewers respectively.

Poetic, elegance, USP and personality copy are liked by 43, 32, 31 and 27 persons respectively. Drama and Exaggeration copy are liked by just 11 and 4 persons. On the basis of liking poetic, elegance, USP and personality copy comes 1st, 2nd, 3rd and 4th as they are liked by 29.06%, 21.62%, 20.95% and 18.24% of the total 148 persons who liked the ad. Drama and exaggeration copy are liked by merely 7.43% and 2.70% of the total persons who liked the ad.

As far as copywise effect of ad on sale of suiting-shirting is concerned elegance, poetic, USP, personality, drama and exaggeration copy influence 22, 21, 18, 14, 9 and 2 persons respectively to use the advertised

Table 5.7 : Effectiveness of ad copies relating to suiting-shirting broadcasted on tv

Sl. No.	Name of Product	Type of ad copy	Persons saw the ad	Persons liked the ad	Persons saw the ad & using the product	Persons saw & liked the ad and using the product	Persons didn't see the ad but using the product	Persons saw the ad & will use the product	Persons saw & liked the ad and will use the product	Persons didn't see the ad but will use the product
1	2	3	4	5	6	7	8	9	10	11
1.	Raymond	Elegance	68	32	7	7	15	-	7	16 -
2.	Siyaram	Poetic & USP	52	23	3	8	3	7	10	2
3.	Grasim	Drama & USP	37	8	4	3	9	6	3	6
4.	Mayur	Poetic & Personality	41	20	3	7	1	5	8	-
5.	Reid & Taylor	Person-ality & Ex-aggeration	14	4	-	2	-	1	2	-
6.	BSL	Person-ality & Drama	22	3	2	-	6	-	1	4
	Total		234	90	19	35	19	26	40	12

Table 5.8 : Effectiveness of separate ad copies relating to suiting-shirting broadcasted on tv

Sl. No.	Type of ad copy	Persons the saw ad	Persons liked the ad	Persons saw the ad & using the product	Persons saw & liked the ad and using the product	Persons didn't see the ad but using the product	Persons saw the ad & will use the product	Persons saw & liked the ad and will use the product	Persons didn't see the ad but will use the product
1	2	3	4	5	6	7	8	9	10
1.	Poetic	S52+M41=93	23+20 =43	3+3 =6	8+7 =15	3+1 =4	7+5 =12	10+8 =18	2+0 =2
2.	Elegance	R68	32	7	15	0	7	16	0
3.	USP	S52+G37=89	23+8 =31	3+4 =7	8+3 =11	3+9 =12	7+6 =13	10+3 =13	2+6 =8
4.	Personality	M41+T14+B22 =77	20+4+3 =27	3+0+2 =5	7+2+0 =9	1+0+6 =7	5+1+0 =6	8+2+1 =11	0+0+4 =4
5.	Drama	G37+B22=59	8+3=11	4+2=6	3+0=3	9+6=15	6+0=6	3+1=4	6+4=10
6.	Exaggeration	T14	4	0	2	0	1	2	0 -
	Total	400	148	31	55	38	45	64	24

Here R=Raymond, S=Siyaram, G=Grasim, M=Mayur, T=Reid & Taylor and B=BSL suiting-shirting i.e. 25.58%, 24.42%, 20.93%, 16.28%, 10.47% and 2.32% of the total 86 influenced persons.

In future poetic, USP, elegance, personality, drama and exaggeration copy will influence 30, 26, 23, 17, 10 and 3 persons respectively to use the advertised suiting-shirting i.e. 27.52%, 23.85%, 21.10%, 15.60%, 9.18% and 2.75% of the total 109 influenced persons.

According to Table 5.8 total number of persons are much more than the actual number of persons because the same persons are counted twice or thrice due to the mixed ad copy used by different suiting-shirtings.

After study and analysis of Table 5.7 and 5.8 it can be said that poetic copy is the best to advertise suiting-shirting on tv. Considering the viewership, liking and influence on usage it can be concluded that elegance, USP, personality, drama and exaggeration copy stand 2nd, 3rd, 4th 5th and 6th respectively. Exaggeration copy is far lesser effective than other ad copies.

To find the composite effectiveness of ads relating to tea, hair oil, tergent powder and suiting shirting the Table 5.9 is prepared with help of Table 5.1, Table 5.3, Table 5.5 and Table 5.7.

Table 5.9 is analysed on the basis of five points mentioned below:

1. **Translation of watching ad into sale**—Out of 896 persons who saw the ads of these four products 239 persons are using these products. That means 26.67% viewers are using the product whose ad they saw. In future 260 persons will use these four products out of 907 persons who saw the ad that means 29.02% viewers will use the advertised product.

Table 5.9 : Composite effectiveness of ads relating to tea, hair oil, detergent powder & suiting-shirting broadcasted on tv

Particulars	Tea	Hair Oil	Detergent Powder	Suiting Shirting	Total
Persons saw the ad	208	192	262	234	896
Persons liked the ad	62	60	90	90	302
Persons saw the ad and using the product	26	27	53	19	125
Persons saw & liked the ad and using the product	23	22	34	35	114
Persons didn't see the ad but using the product	4	9	11	19	43
Persons saw the ad and will use the product	26	32	54	26	138
Persons saw & liked the ad and will use the product	24	24	34	40	122
Persons didn't sec the ad but will use the product	3	9	10	12	34

2. **Translation of liking into sale**—Out of 302 persons who liked the ads broadcasted on tv 114 persons i.e. 37.75% are using the product. In future 122 persons i.e. 40.40% of the persons who liked the ad, will use the product.

3. **Translation of Sheer Watching (excluding liking) into sale**—Out of 594 persons who just saw and not liked the ads, 125 persons i.e. 21.04% are using the advertised products. In future 138 persons i.e. 23.23% of the persons who just saw and not liked the ads, will use the products.

4. **Percentage of users who have not seen the ad**—282 persons are using these four products and out of these 282 persons 43 are such who have not seen the ad on tv. It means 15.25% users have not seen thc ad.

   In future out of 294 users of these four products 34 will be such who have not seen the ad. It means 11.56% future users have not seen the ad.

5. **Contribution of ads into sale**—Out of 282 persons who use the product 239 have seen the ad. It means 84.75% users have seen the ads in other words contribution of ads into sale is 84.75%.

Out of 294 persons who will use the product 260 have seen the ads. It means 88.44% future users have seen the ad, in other words contribution of ads into sale will be 88.44%.

To find the composite effectiveness of every single ad copy broadcasted on tv relating to tea, hair oil, detergent powder and suiting-shirting the Table 5.10 is prepared with the help of Table 5.2, Table 5.4, Table 5.6 and Table 5.8.

Table 5.10 : Effectiveness of separate ad copies relating to tea, hair oil, detergent powder & suiting-shirting broadcasted on tv

Sl. No.	Type of ad copy	Persons the saw ad	Persons liked the ad	Persons saw the ad & using the product	Persons saw & liked the ad and using the product	Persons didn't see the ad but using the product	Persons saw the ad & will use the product	Persons saw & liked the ad and will use the product	Persons didn't see the ad but will use the product
1	2	3	4	5	6	7	8	9	10
1.	Drama	T145+D178+ H62+S59=444	52+68+ 19+11 =150	21+38+ 13+6 =78	20+25+ 7+3 =55	2+8+5+ 15=30	22+37+ 15+6 =80	21+25+ 9+4 =59	1+7+4+ 10=22
2.	USP	T132+D95+ H155+S89=471	48+27+ 49+31 =155	20+20+ 21+7 =68	19+11+ 19+11 =60	1+2+7 +12=22	21+21+ 25+13 =80	20+11+ 20+13 =64	1+2+7 +8=18
3.	Personality	T121+D12+ H89+S77=299	36+2+ 30+27 =95	14+0+9 +5=28	15+1+ 10+9 =35	2+0+1+ 7=10	15+1+ 10+6 =32	15+1+ 10+11 =37	1+0+2 +4=7

4.	Poetic	T41+D100+ H85+S93=319	14+46+ 27+43 =130	6+21+8 +6=41	4+17+ 10+15 =46	0+7+2 +4=13	6+21+ 11+12 =50	5+18+9 +18=50	0+7+2 +2=11
5.	Elegance	T52+S68=120	8+32 =40	4+7=11	2+15 =17	0+0=0	4+7=11	2+16	0+0=0 =18
6.	Exaggeration	T8+S14=22	2+4=6	0+0=0	1+2=3	2+0=2	0+1=1	1+2=3	2+0=2
7.	Promotional	T5+D32=37	0+9=9	1+7=8	0+4=4	0+0=0	0+6=6	0+3=3	0+0=0
8.	Child Innocent	D63	21	10	8	1	11	8	1
	Total	1775	606	244	228	78	271	242	61

T=Tea, H=Hair Oil, D=Detergent Powder & S=Suiting-Shirting.

Table 5.10 reveals USP, drama, poetic and personality copy are seen by`471, 444, 319 and 299 persons respectively. In other words they are seen by 26.53%, 25.01%, 17.97% and 16.85% viewers respectively. Viewersip of other ad copies are much lesser than these four ad copies. Elegance, child innocent, promotional and elegance copy are seen by just 6.76%, 3.56%, 2.08% and 1.24% viewers respectively.

USP, drama, poetic and personality copy are liked by 155, 150, 130 and 95 persons respectively. Elegance, child innocent, promotional and exaggeration copy are 'liked by just 40, 21, 9 and 6 persons respectively. On the basis of liking USP, drama, poetic and personality copy comes 1st, 2nd, 3rd and 4th as they are liked by 25.58%, 24.75%, 21.45% and 15.68% of the total 606 persons who liked the ads. Elegance, child innocent, promotional and exaggeration copy are liked by merely 6.60%, 3.47%, 1.48% and 0.99% of the total persons who liked the ads.

As far as copywise effect of ad on sale of these four non-durable products are concerned drama, USP, poetic, personality, elegance, child innocent, promotional and exaggeration copy influence 133, 128, 87, 63, 28, 18, 12 and 3 persons respectively to use the advertised product i.e. 28.18%, 27.12%, 18.43%, 13.35, 5.93%, 3.81%, 2.54% and 0.64% of the total 472 influenced persons.

In future USP, drama, poetic, personality, elegance, child innocent, promotional and exaggeration copy will influence 144, 139, 100, 69, 29, 19, 9 and 4 persons respectively to use these four advertised products i.e. 28.07%, 27.10%, 19.49%, 13.45%, 5.76%, 3.70%, 1.76%, and 0.78% of the total 513 influenced persons.

According to Table 5.10 total number of persons are much more than the actual number of persons because the same persons are counted twice or thrice due to the mixed ad copies used by different tea, hair oil, detergent powder, and suiting-shirting.

Considering the viewership, liking and influence on usage it can be concluded that USP and drama copy stands first and second. After that poetic and personality copy are lesser effective so they stand third and fourth. Elegance and child innocent copy are just little effective while promotional and exaggeration copy are not making any mentionable effect.

Informatic relating to other non durable goods is also collected. It is presented in Table 5.11.

All the hundred respondents were requested to mention 4 non-durable consumer goods other than tea, hair oil, detergent powder and suiting-shirting, whose ad they have seen on tv. Thereby 400 names were expected and respondents mentioned 389 names of 78 products. It implies very high viewership. Out of 389 names mentioned by respondents 104 are used. Hence the translation of watching ad into sale is 26.74%.

As most of the non-durable products are using a combination of two or more ad copies, it has become necessary to separate these mixed ad copies to find copywise effectiveness of each and very ad copy. Hence the Table 5.12 is prepared with the help of Table 5.11.

Considering the data of viewership and influence on usage shown in Table 5.12 it is apparent that USP, drama, personality and poetic copy stands 1st, 2nd, 3rd and 4th respectively. After these four ad copies there is a big difference in effectiveness of other ad copies. Humorous and child innocent copy stand 5th and 6th respectively. Demonstrative, institutional, elegance, promotional, straight selling and exaggeration copies make trivial contributions only.

Table 5.11 : Effectiveness of ad copies relating to other consumer non-durables broadcasted on TV

Sl. No.	Name of Product	Type of ad copy	No. of persons saw the ad	No. of persons using product
1.	Action Shoes	Poetic	4	1
2.	Alpenliebe	Humorous	3	1
3.	Amul	Poetic & Institutional	9	3
4.	Amul Undergarments	Drama	2	0
5.	Babool	Poetic Personality	2	1
6.	Band Aid	Demonstrative	5	2
7.	Boost	Personality	5	0
8.	Boroline	Poetic	2	1
9.	Boroplus Cream	Poetic & Personality	4	1
10.	Boroplus Ice Powder	Promotional & Personality	3	1
11.	Britania	Personality & USP	5	2
12.	Brylcream	Personality & USP	3	0
13.	Cadbury Chocolate	Humorous & Personality	9	3
14.	Calcium Sandoz	Straight Selling	1	0
15.	Chlormint	Humorous	2	0

16.	Cherry Polish	Straight Selling & USP	2	1
17.	Clinic All Clear	Personality & Drama	5	1
18.	Clinic Plus	Drama	3	1
19.	Close Up	USP & Drama	6	2
20.	Coca Cola	Personality & Humorous	11	3
21.	Colgate toothpaste	Child Innocent & USP	9	3
22.	Complan	USP	3	1
23.	Dermi Cool	Poetic & USP	3	0
24.	Disprin	Drama & USP	7	1
25.	Dollar Under Garments	Personality	4	1
26.	Dominous Pizza	Humorous	1	0
27.	Everest	Drama	7	3
28.	Ezee	Drama & USP	6	2
29.	Fair & Handsome	Poetic & US	5	1
29.	Fair & Handsome	Poetic & USP	5	1
30.	Fair & Lovely	USP & Drama	16	4
31.	Fevicol	Humorous	4	1
32.	Fortune	USP & Poetic	7	2
33.	Jhonson & Jhonson Power	Child Innocent	4	1
34.	Jhonson & Jhonson Baby Soap	Child Innocent & USP	6	2

Sl. No.	Name of Product	Type of ad copy	No. of persons saw the ad	No. of persons using product
35.	Gillete Razo	USP & Drama	7	2
36.	Gillete Shaving Cream	UPS & Drama	4	1
37.	Glucon D	Poetic & Drama	8	2
38.	Godrej Hair Dye	Drama	7	2
39.	Harpik	Demonstrative	2	0
40.	Head & Shoulder	USP	4	1
41.	Huggies	Child Innocent	6	2
42.	Kellogs	USP & Drama	3	1
43.	Krack Cream	Drama	2	1
44.	Kurkure	Humorous & Personality	8	3
45.	Lux Soap	Personality	8	2
46.	Lux Under Garments	Personality & Exaggeration	5	1
47.	Maaza	Drama, USP & Personality	5	1
48.	Maggi	Poetic & USP	8	3
49.	Medikar	Drama & Demonstrative	3	1
50.	Moov	Drama	3	1
51.	Mortein Rat Kill	USP	2	0

52.	M Seal	Drama & Humorous	5	1
53.	Nestle Much	Humorous & Personality	3	0
54.	Nescafe	Poetic & Elegance	7	2
55.	Nirma Beauty Soap	Poetic & Personality	5	2
56.	Nima Soap	Poetic	5	1
57.	Nycil	USP	4	1
58.	Pantene	USP & Personality	4	1
59.	Parle Biscute	Humorous	5	2
60.	Pears	Child Innocent & Drama	3	0
61.	Pepsi	Personality & Poetic	17	4
62.	Pepsodent	Child Innocent & USP	3	1
63.	Ponds Cream	USP & Drama	7	3
64.	Ponds Talcum Powder	Poetic	4	1
65.	Priya Gold	Promotional	3	1
66.	Relaxo Footwear	Poetic & Personality	3	0
67.	Rupa Undergarments	Personality	4	1
68.	Saffola	USP & Drama	5	1
69.	Santoor Soap	Poetic, USP & Drama	3	1
70.	Savlon	USP & Drama	4	1
71.	Stayfree	Drama & USP	7	2

(contd.)

Sl. No.	Name of Product	Type of ad copy	No. of persons saw the ad	No. of persons using product
72.	Sugarfree	Drama & USP	7	1
73.	Ujala	Poetic USP	6	1
74.	Vaseline	Drama	4	1
75.	Vicks Action 500	Straight Selling & USP	3	0
76.	Vicks Vaporub	USP & Drama	3	1
77.	Vim Bar	Demonstrative	4	1
78.	Whisper	Drama & USP	8	3
	Total		389	104

Table 5.12 : Effectiveness of separate ad copies relating to other consumer non-durables broadcasted on tv

Sl. No.	Type of ad Copy	Name of Product (number of persons saw the ad/number of persons using the product)	Total number of persons saw the ad	Total number of persons using product
1.	Drama	Amul Under Garments (2/0) Clinic All Clear (5/1) Clinic Plus (311) Close Up (6/2) Disprin (7/1) Everest (7/3) Ezee (6/2) Fair & Lovely (16/4) Gillete Razor (7/2) Gillete Shaving Cream (4/1) Glucon D(8/2) Godrej Hairdye (7/2) Kellogs (3/1) Krack Cream (2/1) Maaza (5/1) Medikar (3/1) Moov (3/1) M Seal(5/1) Pears (3/0) Ponds Cream (7/3) Saffola (5/1) Santoor (3/1) Savlon (4/1) Stayfree (7/2) Sugar Free (7/1) Vaseline (4/1) Vicks Vaporub (3/1) Whisper (8/3)	150	41
2.	USP	Britania (5/2) Brylcream (3/0) Cherry Polish (2/1) Close Up (6/2) Colgate Toothpaste (9/3) Complan (3/1) Dermicool (3/0) Disprin (7/1) Ezee (6/2)	175	47

Sl. No.	Type of ad Copy	Name of Product (number of persons saw the ad/number of persons using the product)	Total number of persons saw the ad	Total number of persons using product
		Fair & Handsome (5/1) Fair & Lovely (16/4) Fortune (7/2) Ghonson & Ghonson Baby Soap (6/2) Gillete Razor (7/2) Gillete Shaving Cream (4/1) Head & Shoulder (4/1) Kellogs (3/1) Maaza (5/1) Maagi (8/3) Mortein Rat Kill (2/0) Nycil (4/ I) Pantene (4/1) Pepsodent (3/1) Ponds Cream (7/3) Saffola (5/1) Santoor (3/1) Savlon (4/1) Stayfree (7/2) Sugar Free (7/1) Ujala (6/1) Vicks Action 500 (3/0) Vicks Vaporub (3/1) Whisper (8/3)		
3.	Personality	Babool (2/1) Boost (5/0) Boroplus Cream (4/1) Boroplus Ice Powder (3/1) Britania (5/2) Bryl Cream (3/0) Cadbury Chocolate (9/3) Clinic All Clear (5/1) Coca Cola (11/3) Dollar Undergarments (4/1) Kurkure (8/3) Lux Soap (8/2) Lux Undergarments (5/1) Maaza (5/1) Nestle	113	28

		Munch (3/0) Nirma Beauty Soap (5/2) Pantene (4/1) Pepsi (17/4) Relaxo Footwear (3/0) Rupa Undergarments (4/1)		
4.	Poetic	Action Shoes (4/1) Amul (9/3) Babool (2/1) Boroline (2/1) Boro Plus Cream (4/1) Dermi Cool (3/0) Fair & Handsome Cream (5/1) fortune (7/2) Glucon D (8/2) Maagi (8/3) Nescafe (7/2) Nirma Beauty Soap (5/2) Nirma Soap (5/1) Pepsi (17/4) Ponds Talcum Powder (4/1) Relaxo Footwear (3/0) Santoor (3/1) Ujala 6/1)	102	27
5.	Humorous	Alpenliebe (3/1) Cad bury Chocolate (913) Chlormint (2/0) Coca Cola (11/3) Dominous Pizza (110) Fevicol (4/1) Kurkure (8/3) M Seal (5/1) Nestle Munch (3/0) Parle Biscute (5/2)	51	14
6.	Child Innocent	Colgate (9/3) Ghonson Baby Powder (4/1) Ghonson Baby Soap (6/2) Huggies (6/2) Pears (3/0) Pepsodent (3/1)	31	9
7.	Elegance	Nescafe (7/2)	7	2
8.	Exaggeration	Lux Under Garments (5/1)	5	1
9.	Promotional	Boroplus Ice Powder (3/1) Priya Gold (3/1)	6	2

Sl. No.	Type of ad Copy	Name of Product (number of persons saw the ad/number of persons using the product)	Total number of persons saw the ad	Total number of persons using product
10.	Straight Selling	Calcium Sandoz (1/0) Cherry Polish (2/1) Vicks Action 500 (3/0)	6	1
11.	Institutional	Amul (9/3)	9	3
12.	Demonstrative	Band Aid (5/2) Harpik (2/0) Medikar (3/1) Vim Bar (4/1)	14	4

To find composite effectiveness of each ad copy relating to all consumer non-durables broadcasted on tv, Table 5.13 is prepared. Comparative effectiveness of each ad copy is judged by the influence it make on the viewers to buy the product. In this process equal weightage is given to both the four products (tea, hair oil, detergent powder and suiting-shirting) and the other non-durable products.

7.12%, 6.81%, 4.47%, 3.87%, 1.18%, 1.05 and 0.94% viewers use the advertised non-durable as they are influenced and stimulated by the USP copy, drama copy, poetic copy, personality copy, child innocent copy, humorous copy and elegance copy respectively. Promotional, exaggeration, demonstrative, institutional and straight selling copies make just trivial effect. In all 26.68% viewers use the advertised consumer non-durables.

The overall translation of watching ad into sale shown here in Table 5.13 is very slightly higher than the actual figures shown in Table 5.9 and 5.11. This is because the overall translation of watching ad into sale here is calculated by the summation of influence of each ad copy and in calculation of separate influence of each ad copy the same persons may be counted twice or thrice due to the mixed ad copy used by several products.

USP copy is the most effective ad copy followed by drama copy, poetic copy and personality copy. It's effectiveness is 4.55% more than drama copy, 59.28% more than poetic copy and 83.98% more than personality copy.

Just like non-durable consumer goods facts, information and data relating to the four durable consumer goods namely mobile, motorcycle, washing machine and television are collected through the

Table 5.13 : Effectiveness of ad copies relating to all consumer non-durable broadcasted on tv

Sl. No.	Type of ad copy	Copywise %tage of viewers who saw the ad of mobile, M. cycle, washing machine & tv*	Copywise translation of watching ad into sale of mobile, motorcycle, washing machine & tv (in percentage)*	Ad influenced users of mobile, motorcycle, washing machine & tv (3×4/100)	Copywise percentage of viewers who saw the ad of other consumer durables +	Copywise translation of watching ad into sale of other consumer durables (in percentage)+	Ad influenced users of other consumer durables [(6×7)/100]	Average ad influence users [(5+8)/2]
1	2	3	4	5	6	7	8	9
1.	USP	26.53	27.18	7.21	26.16	26.86	7.03	7.12
2.	Drama	25.01	29.95	7.49	22.42	27.33	6.13	6.81
3.	Poetic	17.97	27.27	4.90	15.25	26.47	4.04	4.47
4.	Personality	16.85	21.07	3.55	16.89	24.78	4.19	3.87
5.	Child Innocent	3.56	28.57	1.02	4.63	29.03	1.34	1.18
6.	Elegance	6.76	23.33	1.58	1.05	28.57	0.30	0.94
7.	Humorous	-	-	-	7.62	27.45	2.09	1.05

8.	Promotional	2.08	32.43	0.67	0.90	33.33	0.30	0.49
9.	Exaggeration	1.24	13.64	0.17	0.75	20	0.15	0.16
10.	Demonstrative	-	-	-	2.09	28.57	0.60	0.30
11.	Institutional	-	-	-	1.34	33.33	0.45	0.22
12.	Straight	-	-	-	0.90	16.67	0.15	0.07
	Total	100		26.59	100		26.77	26.68

*Pettentage are calculated from the data of Table 5.10.
+Percentage are calculated from the data of Table 5.12.

schedules. Here in after productwise facts, information data and their analysis is presented.

MOBILE PHONE (HANDSETS)

Information relating to the ads of mobile phone collected from the schedules are presented in Table 5.14. Respondents mentioned four brands of mobile phone that they have seen on tv. These brands mostly used following kind of ad copy prior to and during the research period. Description of these ads will help m understanding their analysis.

Nokia

Its ads are presented with different songs or jingles e.g. '*Dikhane Wali Chij ha to duniya dikhayagi*', '*Jab bhi chhaya tera jado*' etc. In a poetic background one or another unique quality or feature of Nokia is emphasised e.g. the one touch photo phone with which one can take several snaps in few seconds, the low priced colour phones that can be afforded by anyone, Pre-loaded attractive ringtones etc.

LG Mobile

LG uses USP copy to advertise mobile phones. It highlights one distinct and novel feature of LG Mobiles e.g. digital camera for high quality clear pictures, FM radio, MP3 for recording and listening solid music etc.

Samsung

It uses poetic and USP copy. The jingle '*khul ke hai jindgi*' is played and different persons enjoy using Samsung Flip-Top Phone. In another ad a unique safety system is highlighted that protects from loss of theft.

Motorola

Parents suspect their son when they find Moto Flip handset from his pocket considering that he must be doing something wrong that's why he could bought such a costly mobile phone. Mota Flip looks rich but it is available at very affordable price of nearly 3500 Rs.

Film actor Abhishek Bachhan stmis dancing once he listen the rocking music on Motorola's Motorockor Phone even in very serious film shoots.

During research all the 100 respondents were requested to fill 4 blank spaces with the name of mobile phone whose ad they have seen on tv. Thereby 400 names were expected but respondents could mention just 193 names.

According to Table 5.14 out of 63 respondents who are using the mobile of mentioned four brands just 10 are such who have not seen any ad on tv and still using it. In future out of 73 users just 6 such persons will be there.

In all 53 persons and using and 67 persons will use the mobile whose ad they have seen on tv. It implies that the ads will contribute in future to increase sale by 26.42%.

As far as these four brands are concerned, tv ads are contributing 84.13% to the sale, and in future ads will contribute 91.78% to the sale. Thus the influence of ad both at present and in future is highly positive.

As most of the mobile brands are using a combination of two or more ad copies, it has become necessary to separate these mixed ad copies to find the copywise effectiveness of each and every ad copy. Hence Table 5.15 is prepared with the help of Table 5.14.

Table 5.14: Effectiveness of Ad copies relating to mobile phone broasted on tv

Sl. No.	Name of Product	Type of ad copy	Persons saw the ad	Persons liked the ad	Persons saw the ad & using the product	Persons saw & liked the ad and using the product	Persons didn't see the ad but using the product	Persons saw the ad & will use the product	Persons saw & liked the ad and will use the product	Persons didn't see the ad but will use the product
1	2	3	4	5	6	7	8	9	10	11
1.	Nokia	Poetic & USP	72	43	12	2	13	24	2	
2.	LG	USP	49	15	2	4	4	3	6	2
3.	Samsung	Poetic & USP	45	20	4	6	3	5	8	1
4.	Motorola	Drama, USP & Personality	27	1	3	1	3	1	3	5 1
	Total		193	90	19	34	10	24	43	6

Table 5.15 reveals USP; poetic, drama and personality copy are seen by 193, 117, 27 and 27 persons respectively. In other words they are seen by 53.02%, 32.14%, 7.42% and 7.42% viewers respectively. USP, poetic, drama and personality copies are liked by 90, 63 and 12-12 persons respectively. On the basis of liking USP and poetic copy comes 1st and 2nd as they are liked by 50.85% and 35.59% of total 177 persons who liked the ads. Drama and personality copy jointly come yd as each copy is liked by 6.78% of the total 177 persons who liked the ads.

As far as copywise effect of ad on sale of mobile is concerned USP, drama and personality copies influence 53, 43, 4-4 persons respectively to use the advertised mobile i.e. 50.96%, 41.34%, 3.85% and 3.85% of the total 104 influenced persons.

In future USP, poetic, drama and personality copy will influence 67, 50, 8-8 persons respectively to use the advertised mobile i.e. 50.37%, 37.59%, 6.02%-6.02% of the total 133 influenced persons.

Here is analysis of Table 5.15 total number of persons are much more than the actual number of persons because the same persons are counted twice or thrice due to the mixed ad copy used by different phones.

After study and analysis of Table 5.14 and Table 5.15 it can be said that USP copy is the best to advertise mobile on tv. It is used by all the four brands mentioned by viewers. Considering the viewership, liking and influence on usage it can be concluded that poetic copy stands 2nd, while drama and personality copy which are far lesser effective than the first two copies, jointly come third.

Table 5.15 : Effectiveness of separate ad copies relating to mobile phone broadcasted on tv

Sl. No.	Type of ad copy	Persons the saw ad	Persons liked the ad	Persons saw the ad & using the product	Persons saw & liked the ad and using the product	Persons didn't see the ad but using the product	Persons saw the ad & will use the product	Persons saw & liked the ad and will use the product	Persons didn't see the ad but will use the product
1	2	3	4	5	6	7	8	9	10
1.	Poetic	N72+S45=117	43+20 =63	12+4 =16	21+6 =27	2+3=5	13+5 =18	24+8 =32	2+1=3
2.	USP	N72+S45+LG 49+M27=193	43+20+ 15+12= 90	12+4+2 +1=19	21+6+4 +3=34	2+3+4+ 1=10	13+5+3 +3=24	24+8+6 +5=43	2+1+2+ 1=6
3.	Drama	M27	12	1	3	1	3	5	1
4.	Personality	M27	12	1	3	1	3	5	1
Total		364	177	37	67	17	48	85	11

Here N=Nokia, S=Samsung & M=Motorola

MOTOR CYCLE

Informations relating to motorcycles' ads collected from the schedules are presented in Table 5.16. Respondents mentioned four brands of motorcycle that they have seen on tv. These brands mostly used following kind of ad copy prior to and during the research period. Description of these ads will help in understanding their analysis.

Hero Honda

It uses poetic, drama and USP copy. The song '*Hero Honda Shararat, Najakat, Mohabbat, 'isi say aray yehi to hai desh ki dhedkan*' is played in the ad of Hero Honda. In the ad of Hero Honda CD Deluxe the song '*Pant bhi deluxe, shirt bhi deluxe, wife bhi deluxe, Tomy bhi deluxe, ab bike bhi deluxe to life bhi deluxe*'. The deluxe headlight, deluxe graphics and looks are emphasised.

In the ad of Hero Honda Super Splendor the song '*Sarv Shakti, Sarv Suvidha, Sarv Gun Sampan Vijaye*' is played and the unique quantum core engine is presented as extremely powerful.

In the ad of Hero Honda CBZ and Hero Honda Glamour distinct features like alloy wheel, colours and looks are emphasised.

In a dramatic presentation it is showed that the experience of driving Hero Honda Splendor motorcycle is better than the wonderful time spent with a preety girl, in fact it is splendorful.

Bajaj

It uses poetic and exaggeration copy to advertise motorcycles. In the ad of Bajaj Platina everyone wish to look Platina. Even a lady driving a car is highly mesmerised by Platina's beauty and vigour and in the background a film song *'Jalak Dikhla Ja........ ek bar aaja......'* sungs. Bauddh sait performs unbelieveable stunts on Bajaj Discover DTSi Motorcyle. Even a gang of bully-boys feel helpless in a race with one Bajaj Pulsar Motorcyclist. A western rhythmic song is played in the background and at last the slogan fear the black is said.

TVS

Sachin Tendulkar the highest run maker in international cricket praises TVS Victor motorcycle. Attacking wicket-keeping batsman Mahendra Singh Dhoni endorses TVS Star motorcycle.

Yamaha

It uses personality and exaggeration copy to present its ads. Young and dashing film hero John Abraham performs the stunts like Dhoom film on motorcycle. Yamaha bikes are shown as marvelous, sporty and masculine bike.

During research all the hundred respondents were requested to fill four blank spaces with the nine of motorcycle whose ad they have seen on TV. Thereby 400 names were expected but respondents could mention just 216 names.

According to Table 5.16 out of 61 respondents who are using the motorcycle of mentioned four brands just 12 are such who have not seen any ad on tv and still using it. In future out of 68 users just 11 such persons will be there.

In all 49 persons are using and 58 persons will use the motorcycle whose ad they have seen on tv. It implies that the ads will contribute in future to increase sale by 18.37%.

As far as these four brands are concerned, tv ads are contributing 80.33% to the total sale and in future ads will contribute 85.29% to the total sale. Thus the influence of ad both at present and in future is highly positive.

As most of the motorcycle brands are using a combination of two or more ad copies, it has become necessary to separate these mixed ad copies to find the copywise effectiveness of each and every ad copy. Hence the Table 5.17 is prepared with the help of Table 5.16.

Table 5.17 reveals poetic, drama, USP, exaggeration and personality copy are seen by 145, 84, 84, 80 and 71 persons respectively. In other words they are seen by 31.25%,18.10%,18.10%,17.25% and 15.30% viewers respectively.

Poetic, exaggeration, personality, drama and USP copies are liked by 67, 29, 21 and 43-43 persons respectively. On the basis of liking poetic copy is the best as it is liked by 33% of the total 203 persons who liked the ads. Drama and USP copies jointly come second as, both are liked by 21.19%-21.19% of the total 203 persons who liked the ads. After that exaggeration and personality copies are liked by 14.28% and 10.34% persons respectively.

As far as copywise effect of ad on sale of motorcycle is concerned poetic, exaggeration, personality, drama and USP copies influence 38. 15, 11, 25-25 persons respectively to use the advertised motorcycle i.e. 33.33%, 13.16%, 9.65% and 20.90%-20.90% of the total 114 influenced persons.

In future poetic, exaggeration, personality, drama and USP copies will influence 45, 21, 12 and 28-28

Table 5.16 : Effectiveness of ad copies relating to motor cycle broadcasted on tv

Sl. No.	Name of Product	Type of ad copy	Persons saw the ad	Persons liked the ad	Persons saw the ad & using the product	Persons saw & liked the ad and using the product	Persons didn't see the ad but using the product	Persons saw the ad & will use the product	Persons saw & liked the ad and will use the product	Persons didn't see the ad but will use the product
1	2	3	4	5	6	7	8	9	10	11
1.	Hero Honda	Poetic, Drama & USP	84	43	3	22	3	4	24	3
2.	Bajaj	Poetic & Exaggertion	61	24	2	11	4	2	15	5
3.	TVS	Persona-lity	52	16	2	7	3	2	6	2
4.	Yamaha	Persona-lity & Exaggertion	19	5	1	1	2	2	2	1
	Total		216	88	8	41	12	10	47	11

Table 5.17 : Effectiveness of separate ad copies relating to motorcycle broadcasted on tv

Sl. No.	Type of ad copy	Persons the saw ad	Persons liked the ad	Persons saw the ad & using the product	Persons saw & liked the ad and using the product	Persons didn't see the ad but using the product	Persons saw the ad & will use the product	Persons saw & liked the ad and will use the product	Persons didn't see the ad but will use the product
1	2	3	4	5	6	7	8	9	10
1.	Poetic	H84+B61=145	43+24 =57	3+2=5	22+11 =33	3+4=7	4+2=6	24+15 =39	3+5=8
2.	Exaggeration	B61+Y19=80	24+5 =29	2+1=3	11+1 =12	4+2=6	2+2=4	15+2 =17	5+1=6
3.	Personality	T52+Y19=71	16+5 =21	2+1=3	7+1=8	3+2=5	2+2=4	6+2=8	2+1=3
4.	Drama	H84	43	3	22	3	4	24	3
5.	USP	H84	43	3	22	3	4	24	3
	Total	464	203	17	97	24	22	112	23

Here H=Hero Honda, B=Bajaj, T=TVS & Y=Yamaha

persons respectively to use the advertised motorcycle i.e. 33.58%, 15.67%, 8.95%, 20.90%- 20.90% of the total 134 influenced persons.

According to Table 5.17 total number of persons are much more than the actual number of persons because the same persons are counted twice or thrice due to the mixed and copy used by different motorcycles.

After study and analysis of Table 5.16 and Table 5.17 it can be said that Poetic copy is the best to advertise motorcycle on tv. It is most seen and liked besides that its influence on usage i.e. sales is highest. Considering the in viewership, liking and influence on usage drama and USP copies jointly come second, while exaggeration and personality copies come third and fourth respectively.

WASHING MACHINE

Informations relating to washing machines ads collected from the schedules are presented in Table 5.18. Respondents mentioned five brands of washing machine that they have seen on tv. These brands mostly used following kind of ad copy prior to and during the research period. Description of these ads will help in understanding their analysis.

Videocon

It uses poetic and demonstrative copy. The melodious jingle 'it washes, it rinses in just a few minutes Videocon washing machine.....' is sung and the whole washing process IS demonstrated in the ad of Videocon.

LG

It uses USP and personality copy. LG washing machines have a unique *Fabri care system*, so the machine gently clean the clothes without causing any harm to them. LG has better *drying system that leaves no water* and totally dry the clothes. Hence there is no need to dry them under sunlight. Abhishek Bachhan endorses LG Washing Machines.

Whirlpool

It uses drama and USP Copy. The table cover/cloth gets dirty just before the arrival of guests. Everyone in family gets worried but the mother confidently take the table cloth and put it. into Whirlpool Washing Machine. The children raise the question "will mummy's magic work?" Mother says yes it works and joyfully spreads the washed table cover and decorate the table.

In another ad some colour fall on the Ajay Devgan's shirt which he is to wear on shooting. Kajol and her daughter wash it in Whirlpool which removed all the stains with 1-2, 1-2 hand wash system. 1-2, 1- 2 system is just like holding cloth in both fist and rubbing it. Later Ajay Devgan come home, put on the shirt and sprinkle tomato catchup on it saying that now it is perfect for fight seen.

Samsung

Samsung Washing Machine emphasizes the silver neno technology which hygienically clean the clothes. It remove all from the clothes and leave them with a unique fragrance.

Onida

A saleswoman come to give demonstration of Onida Washing Machine. She mistakenly start the machine before her boss join her. She call him loudly manager sahib-manager sahib but she could not find him anywhere. Actually the manager sahib was thrown upward by the tremendous flow of water. Suddenly the saleswoman switch off the machine and the manager sahib fall down with a bang. Through this humorous presentation the power of 400 watt motor is shown, which is fitted in Onida Washing Machine.

During research all the hundred respondents were requested to fill 4 blank spaces with the name of washing machine whose ad they have seen on TV. Thereby 400 names were expected but respondents could mention just 213 names.

According to Table 5.18 out of 36 respondents who are using the washing machine of mentioned five brands just 6 are such who have not seen any ad on tv and still using ad. In future out of 46 users just 5 such persons will be there.

In all 30 persons are using and 41 persons will use the washing machine whose ad they have seen on tv. It implies that the ads will contribute in future to increase sale by 36.67%.

As far as these five brands are concerned, tv ads are contributing 83.33% to the sale and in future ads will contribute 89.13% to the sale. Thus the influence of ad both at present and in future is highly positive.

As most of the washing machines are using a combination of two or more ad copies, it has become necessary to separate these mixed ad copies to find the copywise effectiveness of each and every ad copy. Hence Table 5.19 is prepared with the help of Table 5.18.

Table 5.19 reveals USP, personality, drama, humorous, poetic and emonstrative copy are seen by 160, 88, 47, 34 and 53-53 persons respectively. In other words they are seen by 36.78%, 20.23%, 0.81%, 7.82% and 12.18%-12.18% viewers respectively.

USP, personality, drama, humorous, poetic and demonstrative copies are liked by 46, 24, 14, 12 and 17-17 persons respectively. On the is of liking USP and personality copy comes 1st and 2nd as they are liked by 35.38% and 18.46% of total 130 persons who liked the ads, poetic and demonstrative copy jointly come 3rd as each copy is liked is 13.08% persons who liked the ads. Drama and humorous copies are 4th and 5th as they are liked by 10.77% and 9.23% persons who liked the ads.

As far as copywise effect of ad on sale of washing machine is concerned USP, personality, drama, humorous, poetic and demonstrative copies influence 21, 11, 7, 6, 9-9 persons respectively to use the advertised washing machine i.e. 33.33%, 17.46%, 11.11%, 9.52%,14.29%-14.29% of the total 63 influenced persons.

In future USP, personality, drama, humorous, poetic and demonstrative copy will influence 28, 15, 9, 8 and 13-13 persons respectively to use the advertised washing machine i.e. 32.56%, 17.44%, 10.46%, 9.30% and 15.12%-15.12% of the total 86 influenced persons.

According to Table 5.19 total number of persons are much more than the actual number of persons because the same persons are counted twice or thrice due to the mixed ad copy used by different washing machines.

After study and analysis of Table 5.18 and Table 5.19 it can be said that USP copy is the best to advertise washing machine on tv. It is most seen and liked besides that its influence on usage i.e. sales is highest. Considering the veiwership, liking and influence on usage personality copy stands second, poetic and demonstrative copy jointly come third while drama and humorous copy come fourth and fifth respectively.

Table 5.18 : Effectiveness of ad copies relating to washing machine broadcasted on tv

Sl. No.	Name of Product	Type of ad copy	Persons saw the ad	Persons liked the ad	Persons saw the ad & using the product	Persons saw & liked the ad and using the product	Persons didn't see the ad but using the product	Persons saw the ad & will use the product	Persons saw & liked the ad and will use the product	Persons didn't see the ad but will use the product
1	2	3	4	5	6	7	8	9	10	11
1.	Videocon	Poetic & Demonstrative	53	17	4	5	2	7	6	2
2.	LG	USP & Personality	41	10	1	3	3	2	4	2
3.	Whirlpool	USP, Drama & Personality	47	14	2	5	1	3	6	1
4.	Samsung	USP	38	10	1	3	-	2	3	-
5.	Onida	USP & Humorous	34	12	2	4	-	3	5	-
Total			213	63	10	20	6	17	24	5

Table 5.19 : Effectiveness of separate ad copies relating to washing machine broadcasted on tv

Sl. No.	Type of ad copy	Persons the saw ad	Persons liked the ad	Persons saw the ad & using the product	Persons saw & liked the ad and using the product	Persons didn't see the ad but using the product	Persons saw the ad & will use the product	Persons saw & liked the ad and will use the product	Persons didn't see the ad but will use the product
1	2	3	4	5	6	7	8	9	10
1.	Poetic	V53	17	4	5	2	7	6	2
2.	USP	LG41+W47+ S38+O34=160	10+14+ 10+12	1+2+1 +2=6	3-5+3+ 4=15	3+1+0 +0=4	2+3+2+ 3=10	4+6+3+ 5=18	2+1+0+ 0=3
3.	Drama	W47	14	2	5	1	3	6	1
4.	Demonstrative		V53	17	4	5	2	7	6 2
5.	Humorous	O34	12	2	4	0	3	5	0
6.	Personality	LG41+Whirl47	10+14	1+2=3	3+5=8	3+1=4	2+3=5	4+6=10	2+1=3
	Total	435	130	21	42	13	35	51	11

Here V=Videocon, W=Whirlpool, S=Samsugn & O=Onida.

TELEVISION SET (tv)

Informations relating to ads of tv set collected from the schedules are presented in Table 5.20. Respondents mentioned seven brands of tv sets that they have seen on tv. These brands mostly used following kind of ad copy prior to and during the research period. Description of these ads will help in understanding their analysis.

Videocon

It uses personality and elegance copy. Dynamic and versatile film actor Shahrukh Khan proudly states 'Videocon is an Indian Multinational'. It is very aesthetically designed tv having international technology.

LG

It emphasizes the unique golden eye technology so the eyes will not feel any strain or fatigue whatsoever even after watching tv for hours.

Samsung

It uses personality and USP copy. Rahul Dravid, Virendra Sehwag, Harbhajan Singh and few other Indian cricket players get impressed with the digital technology of Samsung that gives highly clear pictures. They call themselves 'Team Samsung'.

Akai

It generally highlights the big screen tv that gives the pleasure of watching equivalent to cinema hall. It presents big Sumo Wrestlers to emphasize the greatness and strength of big things.

Onida

It uses drama copy. Onida tv is so good that every one envy the person having Onida tv. A monster laugh in the ad and says may cause envy.

Sony

Its hi-fi sound system and flat screen picture tube are highlighted in the ads.

Philips

It is presented as a high class luxurious tv having distinct unparalleled technology. Its LCD tv gives natural pictures. During research all the hundred respondents were requested to fill four blank spaces with the name of tv set whose ad they have seen on tv. Thereby 400 names were expected but respondents could mention just 213 names.

According to Table 5.20 out of 56 respondents who are using the tv of mentioned seven brands just 8 are such who have not seen any ad on tv and still using it. In future out of 61 users just 8 such persons will be there.

In all 48 persons are using and 53 persons will use the tv whose ad they have seen on tv. It implies that the ads will contribute in future to increase sale by 10.42%.

As far as these seven brands are concerned, tv ads are contributing 85.71% to the total sale and in future ads will contribute 86.89% to the total sale. Thus the influence of ad both at present and in future is highly positive.

Table 5.20 : Effectiveness of ad copies relating to television broadcasted on tv

Sl. No.	Name of Product	Type of ad copy	Persons saw the ad	Persons liked the ad	Persons saw the ad & using the product	Persons saw & liked the ad and using the product	Persons didn't see the ad but using the product	Persons saw the ad & will use the product	Persons saw & liked the ad and will use the product	Persons didn't see the ad but will use the product
1	2	3	4	5	6	7	8	9	10	11
1.	Videocon	Persona-ality & Elegance	62	27	6	13	1	7	13	1
2.	LG	USP	43	16	3	10	2	4	11	2
3.	Samsung	Person-ality & USP	35	9	3	3	1	3	3	1
4.	Akai	USP	16	5	1	2	2	2	2	2
5.	Onida	Drama	30	8	2	2	-	2	2	-
6.	Sony	USP	12	3	-	1	1	-	2	1
7.	Philips	USP & Elegance	15	6	-	2	1	-	2	1
Total			213	74	15	33	8	18	35	8

As most of the tv brands are using a combination of two or more ad copies, it has become necessary to separate these mixed ad copies to find the copywise effectiveness of each and every ad copy. Hence the Table 5.21 is prepared with the help of Table 5.20.

Table 5.21 reveals USP, personality, elegance and drama copy are seen by 121, 97, 77 and 30 persons respectively. In other words they are seen by 37.23%, 29.85%, 23.69% and 9.23% viewers respectively.

USP, personality, elegance and drama copies are liked by 39, 36, 33 and 8 persons respectively. On the basis of liking USP copy is the best as it is liked by 33.62% of the total 116 persons who liked the ads. Personality, elegance and drama copy come 2nd, 3rd and 4th as they are liked by 31.03%, 28.45% and 6.90% of the total 116 persons who liked the ad.

As far as copywise effect of ad on sale of tv is concerned USP, personality, elegance and drama copies influence 25, 25, 21 and 4 persons respectively to use the advertised tv i.e. 33.33%, 33.33%, 28% and 5.34% of the total 75 influenced persons.

In future USP, personality, elegance and drama copies influence 29, 26, 22 and 4 persons respectively to use the advertised tv i.e. 35.80%, 32.10%, 27.16% and 4.94% of the total 81 influenced persons.

Here in analysis of Table 5.21 total number of persons are much more than the actual number of persons because the same persons are counted twice or thrice due to the mixed ad copy used by different tv brands.

After study and analysis of Table 5.20 and Table 5.21 it can be said that USP copy is the best to advertise tv sets on tv. It is most seen and liked besides that its influence on usage i.e. sales is highest. Considering

Table 5.21 : Effectiveness of separate ad copies relating to tv sets broadcasted on tv

Sl. No.	Type of ad copy	Persons the saw ad	Persons liked the ad	Persons saw the ad & using the product	Persons saw & liked the ad and using the product	Persons didn't see the ad but using the product	Persons saw the ad & will use the product	Persons saw & liked the ad and will use the product	Persons didn't see the ad but will use the product
1	2	3	4	5	6	7	8	9	10
1.	Personality	V62+S35=97	27+9 =36	6+3=9	13+3 =16	1+1=2	7+3=10	13+3	1+1=2 =16
2.	USP	LG43+S35+ Sy12+P15+ A16=121	16+9+3 +6+5 =39	3+3+0 +0+1 =7	10+3+1 +2+2 =18	2+1+1+ 1+2=7	4+3+0+ 0+2=9	11+3+2 +2+2 =20	2+1+1+ 1+2=7
3.	Elegance	V62+P15=77	27+6 =33	6+0=6	13+2 =15	1+1=2	7+0=7	13+2 =15	1+1=2
4.	Drama	O30	8	2	2	0	2	2	0
	Total	325	116	24	51	11	28	53	11

Here V=Videocon, S=Samsung, A=Akai, O=Onida, Sy=Sony & P=Philips the viewership, liking and influence on usage personality and elegance copy come second and third, while drama copy comes fourth which is in fact far lesser effective than the top three copies.

To find the composite effectiveness of ads relating to mobile, motorcycle, washing machine and tv the Table 5.22 is prepared with the help of Tables 5.14, 5.16, 5.18 and 5.20. Table 5.22 is analysed on the basis of five points mentioned ahead.

1. **Translation of watching ad into sale**—Out of 835 persons who sale the ads of these four durable products 180 persons are using these products. That means 21.56% viewers are using the product whose ad they saw. In future 218 persons will use these product out of 835 persons who saw the ad that means 26.12% viewers will use the advertised product.

2. **Translation of liking into sale**—Out of 315 persons who liked the ads broadcasted on tv 128 persons i.e. 40.63% are using the product. In future 149 persons, i.e. 47.30% of the persons who liked the ad, will use the product.

3. **Translation of sheer watching (excluding liking) into sale**—Out of 520 persons who just saw and not liked the ads, 52 persons i.e. 10% are using the adveliised product. In future 69 persons i.e. 13.27% of the persons who just saw and not liked the ads, will use the product.

4. **Percentage of users who have not seen the ad**—216 persons are using these four products and out of these 216 persons 36 are such who have not seen the ad on tv. It means 16.67% users have not seen the ad.

Table 5.22 : Composite effectiveness of ad relating to mobile, motorcycle, washing machine & tv set broadcasted on tv

Particulars	Tea	Hair Oil	Detergent Powder	Suiting Shirting	Total
Persons saw the ad	193	216	213	213	835
Persons liked the ad	90	88	63	74	315
Persons saw the ad and using the product	19	8	10	15	52
Persons saw & liked the ad and using the product	34	41	20	33	128
Persons didn't see the ad but using the	10	21	6	8	36
Persons saw the ad and will use the product	24	10	17	18	69
Persons saw & liked the ad and will use the product	43	47	24	35	149
Persons didn't see the ad but will use the product	6	11	5	8	30

In future out of 248 users of these four products 30 will be such who have not seen the ad. It means 12.10% future users have not seen the ad.

5. **Contribution of ads into sale**—Out of 216 persons who use the product 180 have seen the ad. It means 83.33% users have seen the ads, in other words contribution of ads into sale is 83.33%. Out of 248 persons who will use the product 218 have seen the ads. It means 87.90% future users have seen the ad, in other words contribution of ads into sale will be 87.90%.

To find the composite effectiveness of every single ad copy broadcasted on tv relating to mobile handset, motorcycle, washing machine and tv set the Table 5.23 is prepared with the help of Table 5.15, Table 5.17, Table 5.19 and Table 5.21.

Table 5.23 reveals USP, poetic, personality and drama copy are seen by 558, 315, 283 and 188 persons respectively. In other words they are seen by 35.14%, 19.83%, 17.82% and 11.84% viewers respectively. Viewership of other ad copies are much lesser than these four ad copies. Exaggeration, elegance, demonstrative and rmmorous copy are seen by just 5.04%, 4.85%, 3.34% and 2.14% viewers respectively.

On the basis of liking USP, poetic, personality and drama copy comes 1st, 2nd, 3rd and 4th as they are liked by 34.82%, 23.48%, 14.86% and 12.30% of the total 626 persons who liked the ads. Elegance, exaggeration, demonstrative and humorous copy are liked by merely 5.27%, 4.63%, 2.72% and 1.92% of the total 626 persons who liked the ads.

As far as copywise effect of ad on sale of these four durable products are concerned USP, poetic, personality, drama, elegance, exaggeration, demonstrative and humorous copy influence 124, 90, 51, 40, 21, 15, 9 and 6 persons respectively to use the advertised product i.e. 34.83%, 25.28%, 14.32%, 11.24%, 5.90%, 4.21%, 2.53% and 1.69% of the total 356 influenced persons.

In future USP, poetic, personality, drama, elegance, exaggeration, demonstrative and humorous copy influence 152, 108, 61, 49, 22, 21, 13 and 8 persons respectively to use these four advertised products i.e. 35.02%, 24.88%, 14.06%, 11.29%, 5.07%, 4.84%, 3% and 1.84% of the total 434 influenced persons.

According to Table 5.23 total number of persons are much more than the actual number of persons because the same persons are counted twice or thrice due to the mixed ad copies used by different mobile, motorcycle, washing machine, and tv sets.

Considering the viewership, liking and influence on usage it can be concluded that USP and poetic copy stand first and second. After that personality and drama copy are lesser effective so they stand third and fourth. Elegance and exaggeration copy are little effective while demonstrative and humorous copy are not making any mentionable effect.

Information relating to other durable consumer goods is also collected. It is presented in Table 5.24.

All the hundred respondents were requested to mention 4 durable consumer goods other than mobile phone, motorcycle, washing machine and tv, whose ad they have seen on tv. Thereby 400 names were expected but respondents mentioned just 194 names. Out of 194 names mentioned by respondents 39 are used. Hence the translation of watching ad into sale is 20.10%.

As most of the durable products are using a combination of two or more ad copies, it has become necessary to separate these mixed ad capies to find

Copywise effectiveness of each and every ad copy. Hence, Table 5.25 is prepared with the help of Table 5.24.

Considering the data of viewership and influence on usage shown in Table 5.25 it is apparent that USP, poetic, drama and personality copy stands 1st, 2nd, 3rd and 4th respectively. After these four ad copies there is a big difference in effectiveness of other ad copies. Child innocent, elegance and demonstrative copy stand 5th, 6th and 7th respectively. Exaggeration, humorous and straight selling copies make trivial contributions only.

To find composite effectiveness of each ad copy relating to all consumer durables broadcasted on tv, Table 5.26 is prepared. Comparative effectiveness of each ad copy is judged by the influence it make on the viewers to buy the product. In this process equal weightage is given to both the four products (mobile phone, motorcycle, washing machine and tv) and the other durable products.

7.07%, 4.76%, 3.12%, 3.05% and 1.21% viewers use the advertised durable as they are influenced and stimulated by the USP copy, poetic copy, personality copy, drama copy and elegance copy respectively. Demonstrative, child innocent, exaggeration and humorous copies make very little effect. In all 21.80% viewers use the advertised consumer durables.

The overall translation of watching ad into sale shown here in Table 5.26 is nearly 1% higher than the actual figures shown in Table 5.22 and Table 5.24. This is because the overall translation of watching ad into sale here is calculated by the summation of influence of each ad copy and in calculation of separate influence of each ad copy the same person may be counted twice or thrice due to the mixed ad copy used by several products.

Table 5.23 : Effectiveness of separate ad copies relating to mobile, motorcycle, washing machine & tv set broad casted on tv

Sl. No.	Type of ad copy	Persons the saw ad	Persons liked the ad	Persons saw the ad & using the product	Persons saw & liked the ad and using the product	Persons didn't see the ad but using the product	Persons saw the ad & will use the product	Persons saw & liked the ad and will use the product	Persons didn't see the ad but will use the product
1	2	3	4	5	6	7	8	9	10
1.	Poetic	M145+Mob. 117+W53=315	67+63+ 17=147	5+16 +4=25	33+27 +5=65	7+5+2 =14	6+18+ 7=31	39+32 +6=77	8+3+2 =13
2.	Exaggeration	M80	29	3	12	6	4	17	6
3.	Personality	M71+TV97+ Mob27+W88 =283	21+36+ 12+24 =93	3+9+1 +3=16	8+16+3 +8=35	5+2+1 +4=12	4+10+3 +5=22+	8+16+5 10=39	3+2+1+ 3=9
4.	Drama	M84+TV30+ Mob27+W47 =188	43+8+ 12+14 =77	3+2+1 +2=8	22+2+3 +5=32	3+0+1 +1=5	4+2+3 +3=12	24+2+5 +6=37	3+0+1 +1=5

5.	USP	M84+TV121+ Mob193+W160 =558	43+39+ 90+46 =218	3+7+19 +6=35	22+18+ 34+15 =89	3+7+10 +4=24	4+9+24 +10=47	24+20+ 43+18 =105	3+7+6 +3=19
6.	Elegance	TV77	33	6	15	2	7	15	2
7.	Demonstrative	W53	17	4	5	2	7	6	2
8.	Humorous	W34	12	2	4	0	3	5	0
	Total	1588	626	99	257	65	133	301	56

Here Mob=Mobile, M=Motorcycle, W=Washing Machine

Table 5.24 : Effectiveness of ad copies relating to other consumer durables broadcasted on tv

Sl. No.	Name of Product	Type of ad copy the ad	No.of Number of persons saw product	No. of persons using
1.	Aqua Gaurd	Demonstrative & Child Innocent	5	2
2.	Asian paint	Poetic, Drama & USP	7	2
3.	Bajaj Fan	Exaggeration	5	0
4.	Binani Cement	Personality	4	0
5.	Bangur Cement	USP	3	0
6.	Birla White	Drama & USP	4	1
7.	Carrier AC	USP	3	0
8.	Dulux Paint	Poetic & USP	1	0
9.	Godrej Storewell	Poetic	3	0
10.	Godrej Refrigerator	USP	7	2
11.	Hawkins Cooker	Poetic & USP	11	3
12.	Innova Car	Personality	4	0
13.	Hero Cycle	Personality & Exaggeration	3	1
14.	Jaguar Bath Fittings	Humorous & Elegance	2	0
15.	JK Laxmi Cement	Humorous	3	1
16.	Kent RO Water Purifier	Personality & USP	5	0

17.	Kit Ply	USP & Demonstrative	11	2
18.	LG Air Conditioner	USP	4	1
19.	Maruti Car	Poetic, Child Innocent & USP	24	4
20.	MRF Tyre	Personality & Drama	2	0
21.	Nakshatra Diamond	Personality & Jewellery	7	0
22.	Neelkamal Furniture	Drama	3	0
23.	Nerolac Paint	Poetic, Personality & Drama	3	1
24.	Orient Fan	Drama & USP	4	1
25.	Sansung Refrigerator	USP	6	2
26.	Santro Car	Personality, Drama & Poetic	6	1
27.	Shree Ultra Red Oxide Cement	Straight Selling & USP	5	0
28.	Tata Indica Car	Drama	4	0
29.	Titan Watch	Personality & Elegance	13	4
30.	TVS Scooty	Personality & Drama	12	4
31.	United Cooker	Poetic & Drama	6	2
32.	Videocon Refrigerator	USP	9	4
33.	Whirlpool Refrigerator	Drama, USP & Poetic	3	1
34.	Wonder Marble	Elegance	2	0
	Total		194	39

Table 5.25 : Effectiveness of separate ad copies relating to other consumer durables broad casted on tv

Sl. No.	Type of ad Copy	Name of Product (number of persons saw the ad/number of persons using the product)	Total No. of persons saw the ad	Total No. of persons using product
1.	USP	Asian Paint (7/2) Bangur Cement (3/0) Birla White Cement (4/1) Carrier Air Conditioner (3/0) Dulux Paint (1/0) Godrej Refrigerator (7/2) Hawkins Cooker (11/3) Kent Ro Water Purifier (5/0) Kit Ply (11/2) LG Air Conditioner (4/1) Maruti Car (24/4) Orient Fan (4/1) Samsung Refrigerator (6/2) Shree Ultra Red Oxide Cement (5/0) Videocon Refrigerator (9/4) Whirlpool Refrigerator (3/1)	107	23
2.	Poetic	Asian Paint (7/2) Dulux Paint (1/0) Godrej Storewell (3/0) Hawkins Cooker (11/3) Maruti Car (24/4) Nerolac Paint (3/1) Santro Car (6/1) United Cooker (6/2) Whirlpool Refrigerator (3/1)	64	14
3.	Drama	Asian Paint (7/2) Birla White Cement (4/1) MRF Tyre (2/0) Neelkamal Furniture (3/0) Nerolac Paint (3/1) Orient Fan(4/1) Santro Car (6/1) Tata Indica Car (4/0) TVS Scooty (1214) United Cooker (6/2) Whirlpool Refrigerator (3/1)	54	13

4.	Personality	Nakshatra Diamond Jewellery (7/0) Nerolac Paint (3/1) Santro Car(6/1) Titan Watch (1314) TVS Scocty (12/4) Binani Cement(4/0) Innova Car(4/0) Hero Cycle(3/1) Ken RO Water Purifier(5/0) MRF Tyre (2/0)	59	11
5.	Elegance	Jaquar Bath. Fittings (2/0) Titan Watch (13/4) Wonder Marble (2/0)	17	4
6.	Demonstrative	Aqua Guard (5/2) Kit Ply (11/2)	16	4
7.	Child Innocent	Aqua Guard (5/2) Maruti Car (24/4)	29	6
8.	Exaggeration	Bajaj Fan(5/0) Hero cycle (3/1)	8	1
9.	Humorous	Jaquar Bath Fittings (2/0) JK Laxmi Cement (3/1)	5	1
10.	Straight Selling	Shree Ultra Red Oxide Cement (5/0)	5	0

Table 5.26 : Effectiveness of ad copies relating to all consumer durables broadcasted on tv

Sl. No.	Type of ad copy	Copywise %tage of viewers who saw the ad of mobile, M. cycle, washing machine & tv*	Copywise translation of watch- ing ad in- to sale of mobile, motorcycle, washing machine & tv (in per- centage)*	Ad influenced users of mobile, motor- cycle, washing machine & tv (3×4/100)	Copywise percent- -age of viewers who saw the ad of other consumer durables +	Copywise translation of watch- -ing ad into sale of other consumer durables (in percen- tage)+	Ad influen- ced users of other cons- sumer durables [(6×7)/ 100]	Aver- age ad influ- -ence users [(5+8) /2]
1	2	3	4	5	6	7	8	9
1.	USP	35.14	22.22	7.81	29.40	21.50	6.32	7.07
2.	Poetic	19.83	28.57	5.67	17.58	21.88	3.85	4.76
3.	Personality	17.82	18.02	3.21	16.21	18.64	3.02	3.12
4.	Drama	11.84	21.28	2.52	14.83	24.07	3.57	3.05
5.	Elegance	4.85	27.27	1.32	4.67	23.53	1.10	1.21
6.	Exaggeration	5.04	18.75	0.95	2.20	12.50	0.28	0.61
7.	Demonstrative	3.34	16.98	0.57	4.40	25	1.10	0.83
8.	Humorous	2.14	17.65	0.38	1.37	20	0.27	0.33

9.	Child Innocent	-	-	-	7.97	20.69	1.65	0.82
10.	Straight Selling	-	-	-	1.37	Nil	Nil	Nil
	Total	100		22.43	100		21.16	21.80

* Percentage are calculated from the date of Table 5.23

\+ Percentage are calculated from the date of Table 5.25

USP copy is clearly the most effective ad copy followed by poetic copy, personality copy and drama copy. Its effectiveness is 48.53% more than poetic copy, 126.60% more than personality copy and 131.80% more than drama copy.

ADS WHICH ARE NOT GOOD

All the hundred respondents were requested to mention four products whose ad they do not consider good which are broadcasted on tv. Thereby 400 names were expected but only 8 respondents mention 15 names in all.

Debicure and Morning Walker that use long and descriptive copy were mentioned by 6 and 4 respondents respectively, Dandi Salt that uses long, descriptive and scientific copy was mentioned by 2 respondents and MDH Tooth Powder that uses poetic and personality copy was mentioned by 3 respondents.

One thing is apparent from the facts that long and descriptive ad copies are not effective particularly on tv. The same thing is confirmed when the respondents were asked about the size (duration) of ads broadcasted on tv. Besides that these ads are less believable. Debicure claims to control and cure diabetes, while morning walker claims to control diabetes and reduce obesity. The prudent and rational viewers of today won't believe such catchy but weak claims.

Mahashay Dharmpal the proprietor of MDH himself endorses the MDH Tooth Powder. He is an old man and his teeth are neither beautiful nor healthy so he weakens the product image. The celebrity or the famous personality selected to present the ad should be suitable for or relevant to the product.

SIZE OF AD

When respondents were asked about the size (duration) of ads on tv 68% suggested that the ad should be short, 24% said it should be very short and 8% suggested that the ad should be long. While not a single respondent suggested very long ad. Hence it is clear that ads should be reasonably short so that the advertising message can be easily attended watched and listened.

6 Research Findings, Conclusion and Recommendations

INTRODUCTION

All marketing activities are customer oriented. Everyone today understand that business can smoothly run and earn profit only by providing quality product and after sale service to the customers. With the mass production and intensified competition it has become increasingly difficult to contact, inform, stimulate and satisfy customers. For this task marketers resort to advertising. But to advertise is not so easy, it requires lot of knowledge and skill to develop and present an effective ad copy.

Ad copy includes all elements of advertising message and its presentation, either printed or broadcasted. In this broad sense ad copy for a newspaper includes headlines, subheads, picture captions, slogans, body of copy, pictures, all other reading matter, trademarks, borders, illustrations and visual symbols. Copy for a tv commercial include words to be spoken by the characters in the script, music, sound effects, illustrative material, action and camera cues. An ad copy is the product of collective efforts of copywriters, artists and layout men.

Effective copy maker conceive, develop, prepare and present the ad message in a workable and convincing way so that desired objectives are achieved and ad gives fruitful results. If the ad copy is weak, it will not be able to attract and stimulate the prospects and the ad will turn into a complete fiasco. So it is utmost important for the advertiser to Use effective ad copy. To know which are the effective ad copies that command more viewership and liking and increase sale, the research work is taken into hands.

COMPONENTS OF AD COPY

There are different parts or segments or components of an ad copy. Generally the ad copy contain the below mentioned components, but in few cases the ad copy may not have any one or more component.

(1) Headline,

(2) Sub Headline,

(3) Slogan,

(4) Illustration,

(5) Body of Copy

(6) Closing Idea and

(7) Identification Marks.

KINDS/TYPE OF AD COPY

Generally the ads of different products published in newspapers and magazines and broadcasted on television have great difference in their contents and style of presentation. These ads do not attract or influence us equally. Their designing, pattern, size etc.

are different. Actually the advertisers are using different advertising messages and appeals. They are depicting or showing the ad in different types. With the increasing modernisation and competition advertisers really developed following kinds/types of ad copies:

(1) Straight Selling Copy,

(2) Suggestive Copy,

(3) Expository Copy,

(4) Descriptive Copy,

(5) Competitive Copy,

(6) Scientific Copy,

(7) Educational Copy,

(8) Questioning Copy,

(9) Order Copy,

(10) Colloquial Copy,

(11) Poetic Copy,

(12) Institutional Copy,

(13) Personality Copy,

(14) Humorous Copy,

(15) Emotional copy,

(16) Testimonial Copy,

(17) Exaggeration Copy,

(18) Demonstrative Copy,

(19) Promotional Copy,

(20) Occasional Copy,

(21) Illustrative Copy,

(22) Elegance Copy,

(23) Unique Selling Proposition (USP) Copy,

(24) Drama or Story Copy,

(25) Child Innocent Copy,

(26) Animated Copy,

(27) Mixed Copy,

(28) Full and Original Copy,

(29) Truncated and Reminder Copy,

(30) Tele-Based Copy and

(31) Serial Advertising Copy.

As the research is related with the effect of ad copy on consumers of Rajasthan it was considered most appropriate to collect the information directly from the consumers of Udaipur district. To study the effect of various types of ad copy, hundred respondents are selected on random basis. Their views regarding the ads of consumer durables namely tv, washing machine, motorcycle and mobile phone are collected through the systematically designed schedule. As far as consumer non-durables are concerned, facts and data relating to the ads of several brands of tea, hair oil, detergent powder and suiting- shirting are collected from the respondents. The main findings of the study are given below:

Comparative Effectiveness of Media

In this research effectiveness of different ad copies relating to consumer durables and non-durables presented through three media channels namely newspaper, magazine and tv are studied.

As we know all these three media are very widely used for advertising. They all influence viewers and contribute into sale but their effectiveness are widely different, it is discussed in Table 6.1.

Table 6.1: Comparative Effectiveness of Media

Type of advertised product	Persons influenced by newspaper ads	Persons influenced by magazine ads	Persons influenced by tv ads
Tea, Hair Oil, Detergent Power Suiting-Shirting	65	36	239
Other consumer non-durables	42	20	104
All consumer non-durables (1+2)	107	56	343
Mobile, Motorcycle, Washing Machine and TV	187	37	180
Other consumer durables	52	9	39
All consumer Durables (4+5)	239	46	219
All consumer products (3+6)	346	102	562

As far as the influence of ads on sale of consumer products are concerned newspaper ads are almost 3.4 times influencive than magazine ads. TV ads are 5.5 times influencive than magazine ads and 1.6 times influencive than newspaper ads. There is an exception in case of consumer durables where newspaper ads are as influencive as tv ads in fact they are 9.13% more influencive than tv ads. As far as consumer non-durables are concerned tv ads influence 3.2 times than the newspaper ads. It is very clear that tv is much more effective than newspaper to advertise products and magazine is far lesser effective than newspaper.

Table 6.2 : Comparative Ranking of Media

Rank	Newspaper			Magazine			TV		
	Weight	No. of persons i.e. Frequ-ency	Points	Weight	No. of persons i.e. Frequ-ency	Points	Weight	No. of persons i.e. Frequ-ency	Points
1	3	29	87	3	3	9	3	204	
2	2	49	98	2	21	42	2	30	60
3	1	22	22	1	76	76	1	2	2
	Total		207			127			266

The same thing is confirmed by the Table 6.2 where respondents have given rank to the selected media.

Sixty-eight respondents ranked tv as number one while 76 respondents ranked magazine as number three. Forty-nine respondents ranked newspaper as number two. In conclusion with maximum points tv is far ahead of newspaper and magazine. While newspaper stands at second position as far as the effectiveness of these three media are concerned.

IMPORTANCE OF ADS

Those ads which are effectively presented and able to find place in the memories of respondents are making solid contributions in their product's sale. Heavy contribution of ads into sale of advertised products reflects the, importance of advertising. This contribution will increase by around 5% in almost all consumer products (Table 6.3).

GROWTH OF ADVERTISING EFFECTIVENESS

The influence of ads on respondents to use the product will increase in all consumer durables and non-durables. Growth of around 10% can be seen in consumer non-durables, while growth of around 20% can be seen in consumer durables with an exception of nearly 30% growth in the users influenced by magazine ads of consumer durables. In conclusion advertising effectiveness will grow at good pace so it is handy to advertise more. The details are given in Table 6.4.

ADS WHICH ARE LIKED ARE MORE EFFECTIVE

Translation of liking into sale is far ahead of translation of sheer watching into sale. Ads which are

Table 6.3 : Contribution of ad into sale of advertised product

(percentage)

	Newspaper		Magazine		Television	
	Ads of selected non-durables	Ads of selected durables	Ads of selected non-durables	Ads of selected durables	Ads of selected non-durables	Ads of selected durables
At Present	72.22	82.74	47.37	25.52	84.75	83.33
In Future	74.74	86.97	50	28.57	88.44	87.90
Growth	3.49	5.11	5.55	11.95	4.35	5.48

Here selected non-durables=Tea, Hair Oil, Detergent Powder and Suiting-Shirting
Here selected durables=Mobile, Motorcycle, Washing Machine and TV.

Table 6.4 : Growth of advertising effectiveness

	Newspaper		Magazine		Television	
	Ads of selected non-durables	Ads of selected durables	Ads of selected non-durables	Ads of selected durables	Ads of selected non-durables	Ads of selected durables
At Present	65	187	36	37	239	180
In Future	71	227	40	48	260	218
Growth	9.23%	21.39%	11.11%	29.73%	8.79%	19.44%

Here selected non-durables=Tea, Hair Oil, Detergent Powder and Suiting-Shirting and selected durables=Mobile, Motorcycle, Washing Machine and TV more liked are more useful and effective. The chances of their translation into sale are considerably very high. If an attempt is made to formulate a single rule applicable to all the media channels and consumer durables as well as non-durables by summing up the data, it will give misleading and inappropriate results because the higher effectiveness of translation of liking into sale differs widely from product to product and media to media ranging from 40% to 300%. But it is certain that if the effective ad copies recommended hereinafter for every product and media category is made, it will be more liked and will influence more prospects.

SIZE OF ADS

In newspaper

Forty-four percent respondents suggested that the ad should be of less than quarter page, 35% said is should be quarter page, 12% said it should be halt page and 9% suggested that it should be of full page.

Newspaper is read just once and that too in a hurry so the readers don't have time to read big and lengthy ads. People read newspapers not for ads but for the news and informations so they just turn over or switch to the next page as soon as they see full page covered with ad. Hence it is wise to place the ads among news and that is only possible when the size of ad is short. Very short ads even go unnoticed so they should be reasonably short or quarter page.

In magazine

Thirty-one percent respondents suggested that the ad should be of full page, 27% said it should be half page, 24% said it should be quarter page and 18% suggested that it should be of less than quarter page.

Magazines are generally read in leisure so the readers may give enough time and attention to the bigger ads and carefully read the whole ad. Bigger ads are more catchy and attractive. Even when a magazine is read again, a cursory look of a big illustrative ad can make a memorable picture in the mind of reader.

On TV

Sixty-eight percent respondents suggested that ad should be short, 24% said it should be very short, 8% suggested that it should be long and no one suggested very long ad.

Generally entertainment programmes are seen on tv so the viewers do not like ad of long duration, they want the ad to be completed shortly. Today multi channel facility is available, if long ad is broadcasted viewer will quickly switch to some other channel and start watching something else. The same thing will happen if several ads are broad casted in a row. Besides that if the ad is too short it won't be able to convey the advertising message convincingly so the ad should be reasonably short.

THE MEMORABILITY OF SLOGANS

Table 6.5 reveals there was none who could not recognize any slogan or pharase. This is a significant indication showing the popularity of slogans which can be handy for popularizing the product. 47% respondents recognize 5 to 8 slogans out of 32 stated slogans. It implies slogans find place in the memories of prospectus so it is effective to advertise using slogans.

Table 6.5 : Memorability of slogans

Sl. No.	No. of Slogans/ Pharases	Persons who rightly associated the product name
1.	1-4	38
2.	5-8	47
3.	9-12	9
4.	13-16	5
5.	17-20	1
6.	21 and above	-
		100

AD CONIES EFFECTIVE FOR CONSUMER NON-DURABLES

Comparative effectiveness of each ad copy is judged by the influence it make on the viewers to buy the advertised product. In this process equal weight is given to both, the selected products (tea, hair oil, detergent powder and suiting-shirting) and all other non-durable products.

In newspaper

Illustrative, straight selling, USP, promotional and personality copies are effective as they influence 37.06%, 24.75%, 13.54%, 7.62% and 7.33% of all influenced users respectively.

In magazine

Illustrative, USP, personality and descriptive copies are effective as they influence 37.78%, 19.18%, 18.80% and 11.08% of all influenced users respectively.

On TV

USP, drama, poetic and personality copies are effective as they influence 26.69%, 25.52%, 16.75% and 14.51% of all influenced users respectively.

(A) Ad Copies effective for tea

(i) **In newspaper**—Illustrative, promotional, personality and straight selling copies are effective as they influence 39.13%, 26.09%, 21.74% and 13.04% of all influenced users respectively.

(ii) **In magazine**—Illustrative, personality and promotional copy are effective as they influence 55.56%, 33.33% and 11.11% of all influenced users respectively.

(iii) **On TV**—Drama, USP, personality and poetic copy are effective as they influence 32.28%, 30.71%, 22.84% and 7.87% of all influenced users respectively.

(B) Ad Copies effective for hair oil

(i) **In newspaper**—Illustrative, USP, personality and descriptive copies are effective as they influence 33.33%, 33.33%, 6.67% and 16.67% of all influenced users respectively.

(ii) **In magazine**—Personality, USP and illustrative copies are effective as they influence 41.93%, 25.81% and 19.35% of all influenced users respectively.

(iii) **On TV**—USP, drama, personality and poetic copies are effective as they influence 41.24%, 20.62%,19.59% and 18.55% of all influenced users respectively.

(C) Ad Copies effective for Detergent Powder

(i) In newspaper—Illustrative, straight selling, USP, and truncated copies are effective as they influence 26.32%, 26.32%, 23.68% and 23.68% of all influenced users respectively.

(ii) In magazine—Illustrative, straight selling and USP copies are effective as they influence 46.67%, 33.33% and 20% of all influenced users respectively.

(iii) On TV—Drama, poetic, USP and child innocent copies are effective as they influence 38.89%, 23.45%, 19.14% and 11.11% of all influenced users respectively.

(D) Ad Copies effective for Suiting-Shirting

(i) In newspaper—Only straight selling and illustrative copies are remembered by the respondents and they are equally effective.

(ii) In magazine—Only illustrative copy is remembered by the respondents and it is quite effective.

(iii) On TV—Elegance, poetic, USP, personality and drama copies are effective as they influence 25.58%, 24.42%, 20.93%, 16.28% and 10.47% of all influenced users respectively.

AD COPIES OF EFFECTIVENESS FOR CONSUMER DURABLES

Comparative effectiveness of each ad copy is judged by the influence it make on the viewers to buy the advertised product. In this process equal weight is given to both, the selected products (mobile, motorcycle, washing machine and tv) and all other durable products.

(i) **In newspaper**—Promotional, descriptive, illustrative, USP and personality copies are effective as they influence 33.10%, 24.70%, 19.35%, 11.58% and 10.07% of all influenced users respectively.

(ii) **In magazine**—Illustrative, descriptive and USP copies are effective as they influence 43.90%, 31.40% and 18.38% of all influenced users respectively.

(iii) **On TV**—USP, poetic, personality and drama copies are effective as they influence 32.43%, 21.83%, 14.31% 13.99% of all influenced users respectively.

(A) Ad Copies effective for Mobile Phone

(i) **In newspaper**—Descriptive, promotional and USP copies are effective as they influence 47.92%, 32.29% and 9.37% of all influenced users respectively.

(ii) **In magazine**—Illustrative, promotional and descriptive copies are effective as they influence 34.89%, 30.23% and 30.23% of all influenced users respectively.

(iii) **On TV**—USP and poetic copies are effective as they influence 50.96% and 41.34% of all influenced users respectively.

(B) Ad Copies effective for Motorcycle

(i) **In newspaper**—Promotional, illustrative, descriptive and USP copies are effective as they influence 34.68%, 22.58%, 18.55% and 13.71% of all influenced users respectively.

(ii) In magazine—Only illustrative, USP and descriptive copies are remembered by respondents and they are equally effective.

(iii) On TV—Poetic, drama, USP, exaggeration and personality copies are effective as they influence 33.33%, 20.90%, 20.90%, 13.16% and 9.65% of all influenced users respectively.

(C) Ad Copies effective for Washing Machine

(i) In newspaper—Promotional, descriptive, USP and illustrative copies are effective as they influence 37.68%, 23.19%, 20.29% and 17.39% of all influenced users respectively.

(ii) In magazine—Illustrative, descriptive and USP copies are effective as they influence 41.18%, 41.18% and 17.64% of all influenced users respectively.

(iii) On TV—USP, personality, poetic, demonstrative, drama and humorous copies are effective as they influence 33.33%, 17.46%, 14.29%, 14.29%, 11.11%, and 9.52% of all influenced users respectively.

(D) Ad Copies effective for TV Sets

(i) In newspaper—Promotional, illustrative, descriptive and personality copies are effective as they influence 29.35%, 27.17%, 21.74% and 18.48% of all influenced users respectively.

(ii) In magazine—Only illustrative, USP and descriptive copies are remembered by the respondents and they are equally effective.

and illustrative copies influence 47.92%, 32.29%, 9.37%, 6.25% and 4.17% of all influenced viewers.

As far as ads of tea broadcasted on tv are concerned drama, USP, personality, poetic, elegance, exaggeration and promotional copies influence 32.28%, 30.71%, 22.84%, 7.87%, 4.72%, 0.79% and 0.79% of all influenced viewers. Similarly with other products we can easily find big difference in the influence of different ad copies. Hence the hypothesis "The influence of different ad copy on consumers is not similar" is accepted.

"Same type of ad copy can not be useful for print and for television media"

In newspaper and magazine illustrative copy is the best to advertise consumer non-durables ad it's share in all influenced viewers is 37.06% and 37.78% respectively. While in case of tele media illustrative copy stands no where, it is not at all effective. Similarly descriptive copy is very effective to advertise consumer durables in newspaper and magazine as its share in all influenced viewers is 24.70% and 31.40% respectively. While on tv descriptive copy is not at all effective.

Poetic copy is very effective to advertise on tv ad its share in all influenced viewers is 16.75% in case of non-durables and 21.83% in case of durables. While Poetic copy is not at all effective for advertising in newspaper and magazine.

It all implies that same type of ad copy cannot be useful for print and for tele media.

Personality copy is effective for advertising consumer non-durables in all three media channels. Its share in the total influenced viewers is 7.33% in newspaper, 18.80% in magazine and 14.51% in tv. Similarly USP copy is also effective for advertising consumer durables and non-durables in all three media channels. Though it is best on tv but just reasonably good in newspapers and magazines. So the same ad copy can be effective for print and tele media. Though the influence may vary from media to media.

In conclusion same type of ad copy may or may not be useful for both the print and television media. Hence the hypothesis is partially accepted.

"For consumer durables scientific ad copy and for consumer non-durables competitive ad copy are most effective".

For consumer durables promotional copy is best in newspaper, illustrative copy is best in magazine and USP copy is best on tv.

For consumer non-durables illustrative copy is best in newspaper and magazine, while USP copy is the best on tv.

Not a single respondent mentioned any durable product that uses scientific copy or any non-durable product that uses competitive copy, in any of the three media channel. Hence the hypothesis is rejected and it is concluded that scientific and competitive ad copies are absolutely ineffective.

RECOMMENDATIONS

1. Ads are making huge contributions in the sale of advertised product and it will increase in future so it is advised to use ads regularly to keep the product live in the memories of prospects and increase sale.

Table 6.6 : Comparative ranking of ad copies

Rank	Drama			Poetic			Personality			Descriptive			Emotional			Humorous		
	A	B	C	A	B	C	A	B	C	A	B	C	A	B	C	A	B	C
0	1	2	3	4	5	6	7	8	9	10	11	12	13	14	15	16	17	18
1	11	19	209	11	17	187	11	16	176	11	13	143	11	9	99	11	7	77
2	10	16	160	10	21	210	10	14	140	10	15	150	10	15	150	10	8	80
3	9	18	162	9	10	90	9	9	81	9	15	135	9	7	63	9	17	15
4	8	15	120	8	9	72	8	13	104	8	14	112	8	6	48	8	12	96
5	7	12	84	7	13	91	7	7	49	7	8	56	7	17	119	7	9	63
6	6	5	30	6	5	30	6	14	84	6	2	12	6	6	36	6	12	72
7	5	7	35	5	11	55	5	2	10	5	8	40	5	12	60	5	7	35
8	4	3	12	4	2	8	4	15	60	4	7	28	4	10	40	4	11	44
9	3	1	3	3	5	15	3	10	30	3	9	27	3	14	42	3	3	9
10	2	2	4	2	3	6	2	-	0	2	3	6	2	3	6	2	5	10
11	1	2	2	1	4	4	1	-	0	1	6	6	1	1	1	1	9	9
			821			768			734			715			664			648

HERE A=Weight, B=Persons and C=Points (A × B)

Rank	Competitive			Scientific			Testimonial			Colloquial			Questioning		
	A	B	C	A	B	C	A	B	C	A	B	C	A	B	C
0	19	20	21	22	23	24	25	26	27	28	29	30	31	32	33
1	11	6	66	11	8	88	11	5	55	11	-	0	11	-	0
2	10	5	50	10	4	40	10	2	20	10	-	0	10	-	0
3	9	12	108	9	8	72	9	4	36	9	-	0	9	-	0
4	8	9	72	8	9	72	8	1	8	8	7	56	8	5	40
5	7	13	91	7	10	70	7	-	0	7	8	56	7	3	21
6	6	15	90	6	7	42	6	14	84	6	11	66	6	9	54
7	5	15	75	5	16	80	5	8	40	5	3	15	5	11	55
8	4	7	28	4	15	60	4	26	104	4	4	16	4	-	0
9	3	4	12	3	8	24	3	15	45	3	16	48	3	15	45
10	2	6	12	2	12	24	2	19	38	2	22	44	2	25	50
11	1	8	8	1	3	3	1	6	6	1	29	29	1	32	32
	612			575			436			330			297		

2. TV is the best media channel so it is adviseable to use it for advertising the products specially for non-durable products. TV is far better than newspaper and magazine.
3. For advertising durable products both the tv and newspaper are almost equally effective so both media channels should be used.
4. 68% respondents preferred short ads so short ad copy should be prepared for tv and that too should be broadcasted where commercial breaks are not of long duration.
5. Less than quarter page ads and quarter page ads are preferred by 44% and 35% respondents respectively. Hence reasonably short or quarter size ads should be prepared and placed among news, it should not be surround by several other ads.
6. Full page ads and half page ads are preferred by 31% and 27% respondents respectively so as far as budget permits bigger ads should be prepared for advertising in magazine.
7. Believable facts, claims and information should be given in the ad and the presentation should also be believable.
8. Slogans easily find place in the memories of prospects so they should be included and prominently shown or emphasized in the ad copy.
9. Ads made today are of good taste and respondents like them. The ads are decent and following the social norms and ideal code of conduct so any additional law or external check is not required to be imposed on ads.
10. Illustrative, straight-selling and USP copy influence 37.06%, 24.75% and 13.54% of all influenced users respectively. Considering their

higher effectiveness illustrative, straight selling and USP copies are recommended to advertise consumer non-durables in newspaper.

11. Illustrative, USP, personality and descriptive copy influence 37.78%, 19.18%, 18.80% and 11.08% of all influenced users respectively. Considering their higher effectiveness illustrative, USP, personality and descriptive copies are recommended to advertise consumer non-durables in magazine.
12. USP, drama, poetic and personality copy influence 26.69%, 25.52%, 16.75% and 14.51% of all influenced users respectively. Considering their higher effectiveness USP, drama, poetic and personality copies are recommended to advertise consumer non-durables on tv.
13. Promotional, descriptive, illustrative, USP and personality copy influence 33.10%, 24.70%, 19.35%, 11.58% and 10.07% of all influenced users respectively. Considering their higher effectiveness promotional, descriptive, illustrative, USP and personality copies are recommended to advertise consumer durables in newspaper.
14. Illustrative, descriptive and USP copy influenced 43.90%, 31.40% and 18.38% of influenced users respectively. Considering their higher effectiveness illustrative, descriptive and USP copies are recommended to advertise consumer durables in magazine.
15. USP, poetic, personality and drama copy influence 32.43%, 21.83%, 14.31% and 13.99% of all influenced users respectively. Considering their higher effectiveness USP, poetic, personality and drama copies are recommended to advertise consumer durables on tv.

Bibliography

BOOKS

Aaker, David A., Batra Rajeev, Myers John G., *Advertising Management*, Prentice-Hall of India Pvt. Ltd., New Delhi, 1995.

Acharya, B.K. and Goveka P.B., *Marketing and Sales Management*, Himalaya Publishing House, Bombay, 1985.

Alferd, R. Oxenfeidt, *Pricing for Marketing Executives*, Wadsworth Publishing Co. inc., California, 1961.

Antebi, Michael, *The Art of Creative Advertising*, Reinhold Book Corporation, New York, 1968.

Azhar, Kazni, *Business Policy*, Tata McGraw-Hill Publishing Co. Ltd., New Delhi, 1992.

Bangar, R.S., *Sales Management*, Printwel Publishers Distributors, Jaipur, 2000.

Barban, Arnold M., Stephen M. Cristol and Frank J. Kopec, *Essentials of Media Planning*, Crain Books, Chicago, 1975.

Basotia, Vijay, *Marketing Management*, Mangal Deep Publications, Jaipur, 2001.

Bateson, J., *Do We Need Services Marketing?*, Marketing Consumer Services, Marketing Service Institute, Boston, 1997.

Bhatia, R.C., *Business Organisation and Management*, Ane Books, Delhi, 2005.

Blankenship, A.B. and Doyle, J.B., *Marketing Research.* Management, Taraporewala and Sons, Bombay, 1965.

Book, Albert L. and Norman D. Cary, *The Television Commercial: Creativity and Craftsmanship*, Decker Communications Inc., New York, 1970.

Boyd, H.W. Jr., Westfall R., Stasch F. Stanley, *Marketing Research-Text and Cases*, A.I.T.B.S. Publishers and Distributors, Delhi, 1999.

Boyd, H.W., Westfall R., *Marketing Research Text and Cases*, Richard D. Irwin, Illinois, 1964.

Brech, E.L.F., *Principles and Practice of Management*, Pitman, London, 1972.

Burnett, John., *Promotion Management*, A.I.T.B.S. Publishers and Distributors, Delhi, 1999.

Burton, R. Durkee, *How to Make Advertising Work*, McGraw-Hill Book Co., New York, 1967.

Caple, John, *Making Advertisements Pay*, Harper and Row Publishers Incorporated, New York, 1957.

Colley, Russel H., *Defining Goals for Measured Advertising Results*, Association of National Advertisers, New York, 1961.

Crawford, Merle C., *New Products Management*, Irwin Series in Marketing, Irwin, 1987.

Czinkota, Michael R., Kotabe Masaaki, *Marketing Management*, Vikas Publishing House, New Delhi, 2000.

Danny, N. Bellenger, Kenneth L. Bernhardt and Jac L. Goldstucker, *Qualitative Research in Marketing*, American Marketing Association, Chicago, 1975.

Davar, Rustom S., Davar Sobrab R., Davar Nusli R.,

Salesmanship and Publicity, Vikas Publishing House, New Delhi, 1998.

David, W. Steward and David F. Furse, *Effective TV Advertising: A Study of 1000 Commercials*, MA Lexington Books, Lexington, 1986.

Denis, Higgins, *The Art of Writing Advertising*, Advertising Publications Inc., Chicago, 1965.

Divita, S.F., *Advertising and the Public Interest*, American Marketing Association, Chicago, 1974.

Frederick, T. Schreier, *Modern Marketing Research*, Wadsworth Publishing Co. Inc., Calfornia, 1964.

Green, Paul E. and Donald S. Tull, *Research for. Marketing Decisions*, Prentice-Hall of India Pvt. Ltd., 1986.

Gupta D.B., *Consumption Patterns in India*, Tata McGraw-Hill, New Delhi, 1973.

Harry L. Hausen, *Marketing-Text, Techniques and Cases*, D.B. Taraporewala and Sons, Bombay, 1971.

Heighton, Elizabeth J. and Don R. Cunningham, *Advertising in Broadcast Media*, Wadsworth Publishing Co. Inc., Belmont, Calif, 1976.

Hurwood, David L. and Earl L. Bailey, *Advertising, Sales Promotion and Public Relations - Organizational Alternatives*, The National Industrial Conference Board, Inc., New York, 1968.

Jacobs, Laurence W., *Advertising and Promotion for Retailing: Text and Cases*, Scott, Foresman and Co., Glenview 1972.

Jha and Singh, *Marketing Management in Indian Perspective*, Himalaya Publishing House, New Delhi, 1988.

Kotler, Philip, *Marketing Management*, Millennium Edition, Prentice-Hall of India Pvt. Ltd., Delhi, 1999.

Leo, Bogart, *Strategy in Advertising*, Harcourt Brace Jovanovich, New York, 1967.

Lucas, Darrell B. and Steuart Henderson Britt, *Measuring Advertising Effectiveness*, McGraw-Hill Book Co., New York, 1963.

Luck, D.J., Wales, H.G., Taylore, D.A., *Marketing Research*, Prentice-Hall, New Jersey, 1970.

Maslow, Abraham H., *Motivation and Personality*, Harper and Row, New York, 1954.

Mehta, Subhash, *Indian Consumer*, Tata McGraw-Hill, New Delhi, 1973.

Millerson, Gerald, *The Techniques of Television Production*, 6th ed., Hastings House Publishers Inc., New York, 1968.

Morgan, Eric A.G., *How to Do Business in Branded Goods*, Longman Group Ltd., London, 1972.

Norins, Hanley, *The Compleat Copywriter*, McGraw-Hill Book Co., New York, 1966.

Ogilvy, David, *Confession of An Advertising Man*, Pan Books, 1987.

Pearce, Michael, Scott, M. Cunningham and Avon Miller, *Apprasing The Economic and Social Effects of Advertising*, Marketing Science Institute, Cambridge, 1971.

Peterson, Theodore, *Magazines in the Twentieth Century*, The University of Illinois Press, Urbana, 1964.

Prasad, L.M., *Principles and Practice of Management*, Sultan Chand and Sons Educational Publishers, New Delhi, 1995.

Quera, Leon, *Advertising Campaigns: Formulation Tactics*, Grid Inc., Columbus, Ohio 1973.

Rathor, B.S., *Advertising Management*, Himalaya Publishing House, Bombay, 1995.

Ries, Al and Jack Trout, *Marketing Warfare*, New American Library, 1986.

Ries, Al and Jack Trout, *Positioning: The Battle for Your Mind*, Warner Books by arrangement with McGraw-Hill Book Co., 1986.

Ryan, J.K. and J.C. Bake, *World Marketing—A Multi National Approach*, John Wiley and Sons, New York, 1967.

Schramm, Wilbur, *The Process and Effects of Mass Communications*, The University of Illinois Press, Urbana, 1954.

Schwartz, D.J., *Marketing Today*, Harcour Brale Jovanovich, New York, 1973.

Sharma, Bhagwati Prakash, Jain Rajeev and Sharma Jayant, *International Marketing*, Apex Publishing House, Udaipur, 2006.

Sharma, Bhagwati Prakash, Jain Rajeev, *Functional Management*, Alka Publications, Ajmer, 1998.

Sharma, Sandeep and Kumar, Deepak, *Advertising Planning, Implementation and Control*, Mangal Deep Publications, Jaipur, 2001.

Shrivastava, P.K., *Marketing Management*, Shiva Publishers Distributors, Udaipur, 1999.

Singh, D.R., Upadhyay, K.M., Tandon, R.K. and Das, N.K., *Advertising with Special Reference to India*, Kalyani Publishers, New Delhi, 1981.

Sissors, Jack Z. and E. Reynold Petray, *Advertising Media Planning*, Crain Books, Chicago, 1976.

Smith, George Horsley, *Motivation Research in Advertising and Marketing*, McGraw-Hill, New York, 1954.

Sontakki, C.N., *Advertising*, Kalyani Publishers, New Delhi, 1996.

Stridsberg, Albert B., *Effective Advertising Self-Regulation: A Survey of Current World Practice and Analysis of International Patterns*, International Advertising Association, New York, 1974.

Subroto, Sengupta, *Brand Positioning Strategies for Competitive Advantage*, Tata McGraw-Hill Publishing Co. Ltd., New Delhi, 1995.

Sudha, G.S., *Functional Management*, Raj Publishing House, Jaipur, 2000.

Trucker, W.T., *Foundations for a Theory of Consumer Behaviour*, Holt, Rinehart and Winston Inc., New York, 1966.

Urban, Glen L, John L. Hauser and NIkhilesh Dholakia, *Essentials of New Product Management*, Prentice-Hall, New Jersey, 1987.

Varren, J., *Global Marketing Management*, Prentice-Hall of India, 2000.

Verma, Sandeep, *E-Commerce, Aavishkar Distributors*, Jaipur, 2005.

Wainwright, Anthony Charles, *The Television copywriter*, Communication Arts Books, Hasting House Publishers Inc., New York, 1966.

Walter, Weir, On The Writing of Advertising, McGraw-Hill Book Co., New York, 1960.

Walters, C. Glenn, *Consumer Behaviour: Theory and Practice*, Richard D. Irwin Inc., Homewood, 1974.

Whitter, Charles L., *Creative Advertising*, Holt, Rinehart and Winston Inc., New York 1955.

Wright S. John, Warner S. Daniel, Winter L. Wills Jr., Zeigler K. Sherilyn, *Advertising*, Tata McGraw-Hill Publishing Co. Ltd., 1981.

Young, James Webb, *How to Become an Advertising Man*, Advertising Publications Inc., Chicago, 1963.

Zaltman Gerald and Phillip C. Burger, *Marketing Research: Fundamentals and Dynamics*, The Dryden Press, Hinsdale, 1975.

ARTICLES

Agrawal D.P., Role of Advertising in Sales Promotion of Drugs in India, *Indian Journal of Marketing.*

Appel, Valentine and Babette Jockson, Copy Testing in Competitive Environment, Journal of Marketing Vol. 39.

Armstrong, Gray M. and Frederick A., Detecting Deception in Advertising, *MSU Business Tonics.* Vol. 23.

Arndt, John, Research into Marketing, *European Journal of Marketing*, Vol. 10.

Baker, Michael J. and Gilbert A. Churchill, Jr., The Impact of Physically Attractive Models on Advertising Evaluations, *Journal of Advertising Research*, XIV.

Chance, Paul, Ads without Answers Make the Brain Itch, *Psychology Today.*

Nakanishi, Masao, Advertising and Promotional Effect on Consumer Response to New Product, *Journal of Marketing Research.*

Shukla P.K., Measuring the Effectiveness of Advertising in North-West Region, *MBA Training Report*, Dept. of Business Management, PAV Ludhiana.

NEWSPAPERS

Aprahan Times

Dainik Bhaskar

Economic Times

Financial Express

Pratah Kal

Rajasthan Patrika

Statesman

Times of India

JOURNALS AND MAGAZINES

Business India

Commerce

Eastern Economics Sarita

Grahlaxmi

Grahshobha

India Today

Indian Journal of Marketing

Journal of Advertising Research

Meri Saheli

Outlook

Southern Economics

Vanita

Index

❑❑❑